Invention Stories

Tales from the Inventor

by

Robert J. Bear

© **Copyright 2016 - All rights reserved.**

The content contained within this book may not be reproduced, duplicated, or transmitted without direct written permission from the author or the publisher.

Under no circumstances will any blame or legal responsibility be held against the publisher, or author, for any damages, reparation, or monetary loss due to the information contained within this book, either directly or indirectly.

Legal Notice:

This book is copyright protected. It is only for personal use. You cannot amend, distribute, sell, use, quote, or paraphrase any part, or the content within this book, without the consent of the author or publisher.

Disclaimer Notice:

Please note the information contained within this document is for educational and entertainment purposes only. All effort has been executed to present accurate, up-to-date, reliable, complete information. No warranties of any kind are declared or implied. Readers acknowledge that the author is not engaged in the rendering of legal, financial, medical, or professional advice. The content within this book has been derived from various sources. Please consult a licensed professional before attempting any techniques outlined in this book.

By reading this document, the reader agrees that under no circumstances is the author responsible for any losses, direct or indirect, that are incurred as a result of the use of the information contained within this document, including, but not limited to, errors, omissions, or inaccuracies.

The following are stories written by the inventors, who had permitted us to use them in From an idea to a Product when first release in 2016. Invention Stories…Tales from the Inventor is the second edition of From an idea to a Product.

Table of Contents

Introduction 1

About the Author 3

The Tornado and Rim Pro-Tec 5

Shop Online to Save Time? Thank Mr. Michael Aldrich 12

Dus-T, A Great Story and a Better Product! 21

The SynPhNe Invention Story 24

The Workblade - a Posture-Correct Workstation 38

SimiWeave™ is Far More than a Semi Success 42

Eric Borgos and the AdoptMe Plush Toys Update 44

Attorney-Inventor's Idea Is Making a Gentle Splash 48

Acid Reflux Patient Finds Relief & Starts an Online Business 52

Spray Away Cleaner & Stain Remover 57

Tyga-Box Systems 63

Michael and Ernest Falcon and PLUNGER-in-a-BAG 70

Trongs - Keep Your Fingers Clean 73

The PerfectSeal™ Gets the Stamp of Approval 78

Abigail Forsyth and KeepCup 81

My Tot Clock 84

Why are People So into this RootSuit Thing? 100

The Socket Saver™ 105

Light Phones 114

The Macy Catheter 117

Discovering Teeth Whitener by Accident 121

Holding Cans, Bottles or Anything That Fits! 126

Gyro Heat Technologies 130

The T1 Pro Race Belt 134

The Water Fence - When it Rains, It Stores 137

Glide Bikes™ 143

The Streetzie's High Heel Bunny Slippers Story 146

Solar Powered LED Christmas Lights 154

Hybrid Wind Turbine 160

The System and Method for Restarting a Wind Turbine 164

The Tibbe-Line Can Save You Time and Much More 167

Tennis Ball Dryer...an Eco Tennis Accessory that Saves 172

DippyCups.. 176

Sugru Mouldable Glue – the Future Needs Fixing 181

Terrafugia®... Driven to Fly™... 201

SnapIt Screw 206

Solve Life's Unexpected Marx..211

Tired eyes can't see the Needle Eye? Get the Spiral Eye™ 214

Budwrap - Wear Your Wires..222

TARPKLIP...226

Appreciation.. 231

Introduction

It was that aha moment...

...and it changed their lives forever.

What sparks the inventor's mind?

Deborah Chester had a dream about two tornados hitting her house. Then it happened and she became homeless. Then her husband had a dream. In his dream, the idea for the Rim Pro-Tech came to him.

Now, they are millionaires.

We all get hungry. Snacking can be serious business. Dan Ferrara hated the messy hands from finger foods, so he set out to do something about it.

He created Trongs. They let you get your nom nom nom on without the mess.

And who knew there would be a market for spandex bodysuits?

Colin Grussing figured it out and was a guest on *Shark Tank* with his invention Root Suit. When they asked if he had made any money, he said, "Hell yeah." In the previous year, 10,000 units sold for a profit of $104,000.

The following are stories of invention written by the inventors, because their paths to success may just show you the way.

At the very least, they will entertain and inspire.

About the Author

My name is Robert Bear, host of the Invention Stories Podcast and owner of InventionStories.com.

In 2007, I began working on an invention for eyewear with removable arms. I built my prototype and gave it to a local company to improve on, which they did. I performed a preliminary background check and discovered there were four similar patented products, two of which were better than mine. Curiously, I couldn't find them on the market. I began researching the invention process and learned the success rate for inventions was less than 3 percent. Why had so many failed?

What does someone do when they have an idea for an invention? I had no idea. I found quite a few invention consulting companies that were ready to charge me for help. When I read the fine print, I learned they essentially guaranteed nothing. I believe the best way to learn how to invent smarter is to learn from those who have already found success.

The following are invention stories that have been shared by the inventors themselves. They were originally published in 2016 as From an Idea to a Product, along with a bad cover and no description, resulting in no sales. In May 2021, we updated this book, removing websites no longer in business and changing the book title and cover.

This is our first book, Invention Stories...Tales from the Inventor. To learn more, please visit www.InventionStories.com

The Tornado and Rim Pro-Tec

By Deborah Chester

This is the incredible story behind how a tornado motivated our innovative, wheel-styling, and protection system Rim Pro-Tec came to be.

I woke up my husband one morning petrified. I had been having a dream about two tornados hitting my house. He told me to go back to sleep, and that I had been working too hard. He said not to worry about it, so I did until July 5, just a few short weeks later.

That day, everything changed for my family. What I initially thought to be the worst day of my life turned out to be the best, thanks to this dream. My daughters and I feared for our lives when two tornados slammed into our house in Oakura, a small seaside township in Taranaki, on the west coast of New Zealand.

Petrified with fear, I thought we would die. We ran to the back of the house that had remained untouched in my dream and I laid my body over the children in an effort to protect them. We began to pray for our safety. I prayed harder than you could imagine in the short time on the floor.

I'll never forget hearing that deafening noise. People say that being in a tornado is like standing at the back of a jet engine on a plane or a train flying by you traveling 270 miles per hour. My daughters screamed as they've never done before. We held on to one another, fearing that if I let either of them go, I would never see them again.

The horrifying noise passed, then we laid there for what seemed like an eternity. I remember hearing other voices shouting outside, so we stood up and looked. Nothing could have prepared us for what we were about to see.

Pure carnage. Two feet long shards of plated glass had speared the children's mattresses and pillows. If the tornado has set down an hour later, the children would have been lying in these beds.

My husband, Chris had been working four hours away. When he learned a small seaside township in Taranaki has been hit by a swarm of tornados, he immediately thought about my dream. He attempted to contact us, but all the telephone lines had been knocked downed by the storm. He called a family friend, who lived 10 miles away and asked him to find us as soon as possible.

Our friend was speaking with my husband, Chris when he arrived in Oakura. The police officers said he could not continue on to where we lived, because it was too dangerous. Our friend handed his phone to the officer so Chris could speak to him. My husband begged to let our friend continue on, to see if we were hurt or worse. He was eventually allowed past the roadblock, and still on the phone with Chris, as he approached our location. Our friend had a hard time informing Chris on how badly the house had been damaged. Initially, he could not see us. Chris became distraught.

He thought he had lost us all, but our friend spotted me up the street in a neighbor's house. He told Chris we were safe and sound. We lost all our material possessions that night. The house was ruined and the furniture destroyed. I never expect to lose everything in such a short time, but I had my family, and that's all that matters.

We were homeless and needed to live with friends for the next three months.

As the sun rose, we learned the full extent of the devastation. The brute force of the tornado's devastation affected 60 homes, six of which were beyond repair, including ours. The tornados had come from the sea and destroyed everything in their path as they spiraled inland.

My girls become anxious when the wind gusts, I hope they get better as time passes.

Rim Pro-Tec

My husband also had a dream about the tornados. In it, we had damaged our cars' wheels. Oddly enough, we had lost almost every material thing in the tornados, yet the wheels on the car survived.

We found it strange that we both had dreams of this event within a matter of a few weeks. I believe my dream saved my daughters' lives, while Chris had one that could change our future. We believe we needed to invent something to prevent wheel damage.

This believed this was our path forward. The following is how we turn our dream into a fantastic reality.

Our Dream/Invention is called Rim Pro-Tec

We moved to Auckland, New Zealand soon after so we could settle away from where the tornados had struck. We started working 17 hours a day, seven days a week. We set up a flooring business in Auckland after the move and worked there during the day. Then, we would come home and work on Rim Pro-Tec at night, so we could move the invention to the next level.

We always knew that we were so blessed to have two dreams: one that saved our lives and one that was changing our lives.

Some days were rough having never brought a product to the market before and motivation was a big thing; keeping going was the only option for me.

I remember one day pulling the car over to the side of the road crying, thinking I really can't take or push myself anymore I just cannot go any further, I sat in the car for a while and decided to put the radio on. I don't know why I did that, after all, I did not have time, but I was so pleased I did. At that time, the song playing said, "You are halfway there, living on a prayer" by Bon Jovi. Well, that song worked for me and I had to keep going. I was now motivated again but this time on a whole different level. I just knew that not only did I have to do this for my family, but I have to do this for the foundation I want to start as well.

Months turned into years but we never gave up on that dream we were going to make a difference. We went through several prototypes, different materials, and lots and lots of testing. We eventually found the perfect design and the best material to use and the dream had become a reality. We had a world-class product and one that I am immensely proud of and extremely excited about.

The Rim Pro-Tec system is made up of a base and inner section. If a curb is hit, the inner part will rotate within the outer base to take the stress away from the tape. Rim Pro-Tec is a specially developed extrusion that is easily applied to the wheel with the use of a proven bond tape.

The system is available in silver or black bases and inners. In many cases, you cannot see the product on the wheels. But if you do want some color, we supply 15 different colored-inners that allow you to have a pinstripe around your wheels. Red, green, blue, or yellow -- the choice is yours and they look fantastic.

The product has been designed to fit most wheel styles and has a universal fitment of 14 to 22 inches. If your wheels are bigger or you want a non-standard color, we can make special order sizes and colors.

Rim Pro-Tec is now being sold in several countries and in several outlets and dealerships around the world, including Lexus, BMW, Mini, and Tesla. We also have more than 100 Patents/Trademarks around the world. Rim Pro-Tec has won Global Media Awards from our peers at SEMA and many more accolades from around the world for innovation and the best product.

After becoming close to leaving this Earth, nothing was going to stop me from doing anything anymore (as long as it is within the law and was also Godly). You have one life and I was going to change them for my family and me.

My Inventing Advice

I would advise anyone that has a new unique invention to put in patents. It is very costly over the years as once you receive your full patents you must renew them yearly. Get your provisional patent first, PCT second, and then the full patent in the countries where you want to enter the market. A PCT will give you time to develop your product and enter the marketplace. You need it if it's a new concept as you have to prove your product and the best way to do that is to pick partners with a good reputation to sell and endorse your product. Co-branding is another way as this opens the doors and starts people talking about your products.

Always remember it's not easy to get your invention into stores. It takes longer than you can imagine and, at the start, it is like pulling teeth. Pick your market first, then knock on the doors and keep knocking. There is no easy option or quick route. It is all about providing proof that your product does what you say it does and getting customers talking about how they like it.

Building relationships, word of mouth, recommendations, and testimonials from leaders in the market is a big help to getting your product noticed by the right people.

Social media is one of the best ways to do this, we have found.

For more information, please visit us on Facebook our website at www.rimpro-tec.com or email us at info@rimpro-tec.com

Shop Online to Save Time? Thank Mr. Michael Aldrich

By Michael Aldrich

In 1979, I connected a domestic television by telephone line to a real-time transaction, processing computer to invent what I called teleshopping

Today, it is called online shopping, e-commerce, e-business, and it is a fast-growing, worldwide, multi-billion-dollar business. E-commerce has changed the way the world does business, and this is the story of how it all began.

Preamble

The names of companies change over time and names of technical ideas do too. In 1979, Redifon Computers was a part of the UK Rediffusion

Group of Companies. In 1980, the company's name was changed to Rediffusion Computers. In November 1984, under new ownership, it was changed again to ROCC Computers (Rediffusion's Old Computer Company).

In 1979, there was no such thing as online shopping, so when I invented it, I called it teleshopping... meaning shopping at a distance. Unknown to me, in 1977, a TV-selling technique called infomercials (effectively paid advertising programs on TV with a pitchman urging viewers to make a phone call to buy goods) was also being called teleshopping. Over the years (in USA TV terminology) 'teleshopping' succeeded 'infomercials' and my 'teleshopping' – real-time transaction processing from home via a television or personal computers – became 'online shopping.' The terms 'e-commerce' and 'e-business' are from the 1990s. We never used those terms.

The Beginning

In early 1979, a 26-inch color television set was delivered to my office on the Crawley Industrial Estate, Sussex, UK. With it came a note asking me for my assessment of it. The Rediffusion Group manufactured televisions, so it wasn't unusual to be given prototypes for testing. It just wasn't one of our priorities (we were computer manufacturers), so the television sat in the corner of the office, unused, for a couple of months. During that time, we learned that it was a prototype of television designed for a new service to be offered by the Post Office called 'Prestel.' Prestel was a kind of Ceefax/Teletex service (available on UK broadcast TV providing news, weather, and other text information) delivered by telephone line rather than broadcast by the BBC and ITV. Prestel was to be a paid commercial service (Ceefax / Teletext were free) providing information supplied by independent IPs (information providers).

We performed a little desk research on the Prestel idea and business model but could not see how to make money from such a venture. In any case, we were too busy with our computer business. So, the television in the corner was not switched on.

One day, one of our engineers, Peter Champion, asked if he could strip the television to find out what was inside. This was not an unusual request from an engineer, so I said, "Be my guest."

Some weeks later, he came back and mentioned that he had found a chipset with a chip modem, a character generator, and an auto-dialer that could hold four telephone numbers. As we casually chatted about it, he said, "If we built a controller for one of our computers, we could connect the television (just like Prestel)." At the time, we made real-time computers and visual display units (desktop terminals) for large corporations. There wasn't much demand for televisions from those companies.

That summer, my wife Sandy and I were walking our Labrador, Tessa, in the St Leonard's Forest, behind our house in Colgate, Sussex. We were relaxing, talking about our children, and doing the usual family domestic things. I was thinking that we could use some assistance with the boring weekly supermarket shopping expedition. All of a sudden, I thought about the television and hooking it up to the supermarket so we could have the supermarket deliver our groceries. I told my wife my idea and we rushed back to the house to start planning.

It was simple. We had a domestic television that could communicate and a computer that could handle transaction processing from multiple users and also communicate with other computers. We could build a networked, real-time transaction processing system. Using an inexpensive domestic television with a remarkably simple human interface, it could be used by anyone, anywhere, without training. With its ability to dial into any computer via a normal domestic telephone line and using standard communication and human interface, this could be used for multiple applications. It wasn't restricted to only talking to just one computer for one function, such as airline reservation systems. It had genuine open-market, independent teleshopping capabilities. Also, you could still watch TV! It was hugely exciting.

Next, I did two things. First, thinking about the potential of the new idea from every angle, I wrote a tumble and jumble of ideas into a large number of papers. Some of the papers were eventually gathered together and published as a book in 1982 – 'Videotex – Key to the Wired City.' Second, I asked my inquisitive engineer to 'bodge up' a connection to link the prototype television to one of our computers. It worked!

I didn't know what to do. The ideas of teleshopping, telebanking, teleworking, tele- everything seemed like crazy science fiction. There was no market, no demand, and no infrastructure. Perhaps it was all nuts. We had to get a reality check, talk to real people to get some feedback and reactions. Yet, we had to do it all in total privacy. No one must know what we were doing until we figured out what we should be doing.

So, we hit on a plan. We would take our system to the Data Entry Management Association Conference in New Orleans in September 1979. We would rent some space, then show visitors what we'd done and gauge their reaction. Nobody would know us and we would leave town quickly. Three people would go to New Orleans. I would give the presentation, my wife, Sandy would operate the television, while my inquisitive engineer, Peter Champion, would make the 'bodge' work.

We packed our gear and went. Unfortunately, all of our equipment was 240 volts / 50 Hz. The United States operates on 110 volts / 60 Hz. No small problem, but somehow, we found the conversion solution. When we arrived at the Convention Centre in New Orleans, we learned that we were not allowed to carry in our rag-tag kit of equipment. It was a unionized facility and the union did all the heavy lifting. Fortunately, we managed to negotiate a deal.

Our stand at the exhibition consisted of a table covered in green cloth with the television on top. Under the table, concealed by the cloth was our intrepid engineer lying on his back ready to 'bodge' the connection, at specific moments during the presentation. We were there for three days. It was all a bit cheeky.

It worked. The visitors became intrigued, even excited. They even loved the picture quality on the television. We could have sold many systems. The question we needed answered was affirmed -- they loved the idea of shopping from home. It was a winner! We left no forwarding address as we hot-footed it back to the United Kingdom.

Roger Newman and his team designed a multi-port controller for the TV. Jim Bethel built the complete interface software to run the system. We set a public launch date of April 1980 for our new system. We were going to make a business of online shopping!

We rented a conference room at the Quaglinos Hotel in London, England at the end of March 1980 for our press conference. We announced 'Redifon's Office Revolution.' The Revolution was that heretofore information systems had been in-house servicing corporate needs. Now the corporations were going to connect the outside world (customers, consumers, agents, distributors, suppliers, service companies) to their corporate databases, to conduct business electronically. We were releasing the system that would do it, deliverable in 90 days from the signing of the contract.

The media were bemused, instantly latching on to the televisions connecting to the computers. They seemed familiar with the parts but didn't understand the rest. In hindsight, this was probably the beginning of e-commerce and e-business as we know it today. The product launch followed in early April 1980, when we demonstrated our system across the UK. We re-launched in July 1980 because so few understood what we were talking about.

Building a Market

Except for a handful of people, nobody in the world knew what we were doing. Those that did probably thought we were mad; however, we had a plan.

Most inventions never make money for their inventors. For online shopping, we had to build awareness and create a financially viable product for our clients as well as ourselves. In addition, we had to create a new market without spending any real money.

However, we had some huge advantages. The product development costs were quite low. Also, we had a multi-user, real-time transaction processing mini-computer that was fast, versatile, and relatively inexpensive. In addition, we had a client base of large corporations and public and government institutions. Ultimately, the rest would not be difficult.

We called the new technology 'Videotex' to differentiate it from Prestel. We produced an add-on feature to our office computer called 'Viewdata Plus' because there was free publicity around the word 'Viewdata.'

Because we were only adding our new technology to an existing one (that somewhat enhanced system), we knew we had stability, reliability, and dependability. The system was bomb-proof.

The marketing plan was simple. We would sell our idea to the big corporations who could connect their agents, distributors, and customers to their corporate information systems for direct shopping and sales. No third parties would be involved. We coined the name 'private system.' We divided the big corporations into leaders and followers, then focused solely on the leaders. We sold our 'competitive advantage' to be gained from our new technique and made compelling financial arguments. We shared this beneficial cost/ benefit analysis... and that was how we sold our systems. This idea became known as Business to Business [B2B] online shopping.

Our plan worked like a dream. Soon we were knee-deep in projects. We were the world's first in the travel industry. We were also pioneering in the automotive industry with a 'locate a car' system for one of the world's largest manufacturers. We were first in the car financing systems with automatic checks with credit-rating agencies. Also, we were pioneers in supermarket shopping, services for the elderly, and even taxi-booking services. To avoid spending money on advertising and promotion, we utilized free editorial and conference papers extensively. It wasn't difficult due to the huge level of interest.

The challenges of Videotex came from the telecoms, while consumer electronics were from the computer industry. The computer industry wasn't interested and made only some token gestures towards it. The press was intrigued, but highly skeptical. The net result is that we sold our systems with little competition for 10 years, making excellent profits.

Developing the Market

B2Bs were commercially viable from the beginning because companies could afford to set up their networks or use the videotex terminals already installed in customers' offices by third parties for other purposes. These terminals had programmable, auto-dialers that could hook up to any computer. The human interface was standard, so learning another system was simplified. Some of the early systems ran virtually unchanged into the 21st century.

The first B2Bs became operational in 1981. B2Cs (Business to Consumer) online shopping (as in supermarket shopping) would not become commercially viable until the 1990s. This occurred when a critical mass of installed, home computers was reached. Improved telecommunications with the internet and the world wide web opened up continents when service providers appeared in the volume.

From 2000 onwards, improved availability of bandwidth (thanks to broadband) at affordable prices, improved encryption for payment processing, and improved search engines led to exponential growth in service providers. This resulted in near-saturation in home computers. Many countries made B2C ubiquitous from the first B2C supermarket online shopping in 1984. It took nearly 20 years before B2C became a force in retailing.

The original pioneering work was not lost, migrating to the internet in the 1990s. Reading those original papers again today, the social impact has been pretty well as predicted, even if the videotex technology proved short-lived. Today's internet shopping has gone far beyond our wildest dreams.

For the record books:

September 1979 - The first public demonstration of online shopping

March 1980 - The launch of what was later called online shopping, e-commerce, and e-business

March 1981 - The first B2B, Thomson Holidays, went live.

May 1984- The world's first online home shopper, Jane Snowball, used the Gateshead SIS/Tesco system to buy groceries.

Dus-T, A Great Story and a Better Product!

By Steve Baker

DUS-T is a protective garment with a deployable face mask

Usually, a great product starts from a specific need not being met by the consumer market. This was the case for me, as in my construction trade, I experienced dust on the job every day and dealing with a dust mask became a common problem. I was continually looking for it or wondering if it were dirty. If I had shaved that day, would it create a seal and work properly? Besides being uncomfortable, the common dust mask was expensive to use. I went through hundreds of them in a few short months, making it a financial burden. To save money, I began pulling my shirt over my nose and mouth whenever dust protection was needed instead.

After several years of doing this, I realized there had to be a better solution since this situation must be affecting others as well. One day, a lightbulb went on. I ran home, grabbed a couple of shirts, socks, and some pins, and began to work on a prototype. I cut a sleeve from a shirt just below the shoulder and pulled it over my head. I put another shirt over that one, pinning it just below the collar. I was now ready to start working on the mask portion.

The sleeve made a great start as it covered my face. To make it stay in place, I would have to cut slits in the rear area for loops. This was easy to do and was quite effective. Next, for the mouth and nose cover, I cut the sock at the heel portion that resulted in a round, comfortable solution for the filter. This was easier than I imagined.

Next came the hard part...sewing. I hadn't sewn since junior high, so this would be a challenge. My sewing machine had been passed down to me by family but I had never used it. I threaded the needle and began stitching each area I had pinned. I finished sewing this prototype in about three hours. The DUS-T was born -- a machine washable, reusable, easily accessible mask that deploys in seconds from the collar of a shirt.

I began wearing it daily. After extensive use, I concluded that my invention was the solution to the problem I'd been seeking. If I had this problem, there must be others who would benefit from my invention too.

Wanting to protect my idea, my next obstacle would be patenting DUS-T. Having no experience with this process, it became a three-year odyssey of arguing with the United States Patent and Trademark Office regarding patentability. There were many other inventions it needed to get around, but the DUS-T was my invention and I was determined to succeed. Relentlessly, I pursued this goal until I was awarded United States Patent# 7228858 in 2007.

When you're awarded your patent, the first thing you think is you're going to get rich fast. Needless to say, this is far from the truth. In fact, obtaining your patent is the easiest part. Manufacturing, marketing, and selling your new invention will prove to be the hardest steps, requiring persistence, passion, and hard work. You'll need it if your goal is to sell your invention.

Tons of money, time, tears, and uncertainty will be on your daily checklist while going through this endeavor. Keeping the people around you on board while not losing faith in your vision is critical to your success. I believe this when I began this journey but had to remind myself and the people close to me every day. One day it will be worth it!

Since being awarded my "protective garment" patent in 2007, I have begun filing international patents, with 3 new ones issued to date. I have traveled the globe, selling thousands of DUS-Ts. My invention has been featured on the History Channel and Invention USA. The DUS-T has 10 different designs, has function that ranges from flame-resistant to anti-viral and sells in more than 20 market categories including industrial, hunting, and medical.

The most rewarding part for me is knowing that people everywhere have benefitted from my passion and persistence. You can learn more about and purchase the DUS-T at www.thedus-t.com or www.dus-tshirt.com. See for yourself what many years of work, sweat, and tears have resulted. Thank you for reading my story and good luck with your endeavors.

The SynPhNe Invention Story

By Subhasis Banerji

Inventors: Dr. Subhasis Banerji, Dr. John Heng Institution: Nanyang Technological University, Singapore Company: Synphne Pte Ltd., Singapore.

Background

The world has seen substantial progress in technologies used to communicate with the external world. However, people are becoming increasingly alienated from communicating "internally" with their bodies and their mind. They struggle to find the time and understanding. This has resulted in the reduced capabilities in managing stress, sleep, illness recovery, resulting in chronic disease. The detrimental impact of this on health and quality of life is significant. Healthcare facilities are stretched. We use technology to monitor our heart rates, blood pressure, and sleeping patterns while desiring to bring about long-lasting change.

SynPhNe (an abbreviation for the synergistic physio-neuro platform and pronounced similar to the word "symphony") is a wearable, connected health device that assists you in communication with and coordinates your mind and body. It captures the electrical activity in the brain and muscle then teaches how to self-correct your unconscious responses which may be hampering performance, relaxation, and learning. The self-correction is done in real-time while doing everyday tasks. So far, it has helped paralyzed stroke patients as well as those with high blood pressure and joint pain. Formal studies have been conducted in hospitals with patients who had been given no further hope of improvement, as also in the poorer community where healthcare is inaccessible or unaffordable.

The Idea

In 1998, a car accident left me nearly immobile and in constant, severe pain. My shattered hip was reconstructed surgically, but my thinking remained somewhat hazy. I suffered from frequent episodes of blank memory, unexplained bouts of depression, and an inability to manage stress. Learning to walk all over again was extremely painful. Post-surgery, my affected leg was somewhat shorter than my other leg. My doctors informed me that I may never walk normally again and may require long-term medication for depressive disorder. I began experimenting with deep relaxation, resistance training, joint alignment, and muscle tissue elongation techniques from the martial arts and yoga that I had previously learned and practiced. Six months later, I returned to my doctor's office. I showed him that I could walk without limping, do a half squat, and bend forward to touch my knees, all without pain. You can say I learned to walk again alongside my daughter, Sumona, who was then just one year old.

Over the next two years, I used the same techniques to erase the limp in my walk. I started to run and jump then returned to my martial arts practice. My Tai Chi and Qigong (Chi Kung) training enabled me to eradicate the postural and mental difficulties I had been experiencing. This put me on the road to full recovery, finally free of pain. My depression and psychosis symptoms disappeared and my memory became more reliable.

This incident inspired me to leave my machine design and industrial automation business. At the time, I was having trouble touring around work and spending long hours on my feet. I began teaching yoga and martial art-based therapy full-time. I was happy to be doing, at age 40, what I had always been passionate about. Even though I delivered great results in people with a variety of disorders, it took too long, was too expensive, and was difficult to scale.

As a faculty member at Nanyang Technological University, I knew that technology was needed to address this real market need. But could it be done? No one had combined yoga and tai chi with mainstream medical technology before. What could we measure? How would people learn? What would be needed to bring about clinically significant changes? I was unable to find a satisfying answer in published literature or in the marketplace. Being unfamiliar with biomedical technology, I enrolled for a Master's course in Singapore in 2007. This was where I met my future co-founder and good friend, Dr. John Heng.

A year later I started a rewarding learning journey under my Tai Chi teacher, Master Tek Siaw, which helped formulate the SynPhNe model. The university and local hospital were keen on a robotics project with stroke patients. We incorporated the principles of yoga and tai chi into a bio-mechatronics technological solution for stroke patients with paralyzed arms and hands.

First Study

The first pilot study we performed using nine stroke patients showed some unexpected results. Most stroke patients responded with self-correction of their unconscious and maladaptive muscular reactions within a single session of being guided into it by the software. The idea was for the patient to look at a computer screen displaying electrical activity in different parts of his/her impaired arm, then consciously inhibit certain unconscious muscle reactions. The patients shared that they knew why they had stopped improving. They were consistent, but unknowingly doing certain things wrong. It renewed their confidence in the belief they would one day use their hands. We analyzed the electrical activity data from the patients' arm muscles and concluded the process could be automated into a self-sufficient system suitable for home use.

This was a turning point in the project. However, there was a lot of skepticism among doctors and scientists regarding this approach. The premise that "doing less" would be more beneficial to patients who had been prescribed exercise, and that limb-impaired patients could "auto self-correct" their movements without physical assistance, seemed counter-intuitive.

I enroll in a part-time Ph.D. program to perform a formal, academic validation of the SynPhNe physio-neuro model, the technology, the protocol, and its clinical outcomes. I simultaneously moved out of the technology group and took up a full-time research position at the medical school of the National University of Singapore. This allowed me to study the clinical aspects of movement analysis and aging. John and

I applied and were awarded a proof-of-concept grant from the National Research Foundation in Singapore. Frequently logging 75 hours a week, using tai chi and yoga techniques to manage stress from work and travel, and with John's constant support, I completed my Ph.D. in August 2014 at the ripe young age of 50. The abbreviation "SynPhNe" was suggested by my sister, Sushmita Mazumdar, who resides in Virginia, USA. It stuck as patients seemed to like it and recall it easily.

The Prototype Process

Starting the project in 2007, we were able to establish a first stage proof-of-concept by 2010. We dedicated 2011-1012 to create our first miniaturized, wearable version, which weighed less than a kilogram. We made the software interface more user-friendly, using animals and trees, and smiles to make interpretation and training easier to understand. All complexity, graphs, data, therapy management, and personalization were transferred to the back end. Rather than designing a typical medical device, we designed a device that was more along the lines of a typical consumer electronic device. The guiding principles were accessibility and affordability. We rejected several components and sensors which were readily available in the market but added to the cost. We built a prototype from scratch. We were assisted at this stage by a new addition to the team, P. Ponvignesh, who had worked for several years in the embedded technology industry.

Our prototype weighed less than 800 gm when worn. We tested it on 15 patients in a typical hospital ward under the direct supervision of therapists. We added a new member, Daphne Menezes, who oversaw these trials as part of her Master's program. Only those long-term subjects were chosen for whom no further improvement was to be expected from conventional and robotic rehabilitation. Using SynPhNe, most subjects showed significant improvements in hand use within four weeks, including dexterous activities, such as using chopsticks. The next question was, "Is this enough to ensure people could use it at home?" A system used in the hospital, however successful, would never solve the problem. We received our first round of private funding from friends and family, as well as the prestigious SMART (Singapore-MIT Alliance for Research and Technology) Innovation Grant in 2012. SMART provided valuable mentorship in converting our research project into a viable business.

SynPhNe had its first press release, thanks to Nanyang Technological University. We shared our findings on the internet, receiving trial and patient inquiries from several countries.

Our Second Prototype

Prototype version 2.0 was aimed at minimizing the interventions from a therapist. Data management and the sensor set-up process were simplified. The menu of exercises was increased and our system was made available in English and Chinese. No mechanical assistance was provided to subjects in this version. Ten patients tried it out and the results were comparable to the previous trial. Not one therapy session out of 120 sessions was conducted by a therapist. The results indicated that training with SynPhNe required performing just one-fifth the number of exercise repetitions (5-10 repetitions only per session) when compared to robotic rehabilitation and high-intensity therapy which were focused on a higher number of repetitions; considered the gold standard.

The Final Research Prototype

Prototype version 3.0 was produced a year later for third-party use and remote monitoring. The user interface was significantly changed for layperson use, with interlocks to ensure that important milestones were reached during each therapy session. The remote online support for training and therapy setup was put in place using open-source tools. India was chosen for testing and a Hindi version of the system was created.

This trial, with 30 subjects, is now in progress and the clinician team is considering extending the treatment to patients with traumatic brain injury and cerebral palsy.

In 2014, we decided it was time to start building our first wireless alpha commercial prototype, in compliance with CE and FDA regulatory norms. We raised money using grants (SPRING Singapore Technology Commercialization Grant 2014) and private funding. We wrote our first go-to-market roadmap.

The Patent Process

The SynPhNe project brought together elements from neuroscience, development biology, pediatrics, biomechanics, electromyography, electroencephalography, geriatrics, bio-mechatronics, and embedded technology. It also included fundamental elements of healing from conventional therapy, yoga, qigong, and tai chi. The university initially believed our invention idea would be unpatentable.

The university assisted us in obtaining expert patent attorneys in the field of neuroscience and rehabilitation. It was determined that several claims should be filed. Happily, for us, the core concepts and processes that we had developed had not been disclosed. We had been too busy to write and publish papers. We filed patents for these while keeping certain mathematical algorithms unpublished as trade secrets.

The university subsequently filed for a provisional patent, which was later converted into national-level patent applications in Singapore, China, India, the US, Europe, Australia, and Malaysia. These we the markets we felt we could reach in the next 10 years. In 2014, we were awarded our first patent in Singapore, then signed an exclusive licensing agreement with the university.

Marketing

At first, we targeted this solution at all those "plateaued" stroke patients with impaired hand function, whom mainstream doctors and hospitals have given up on. We planned to accomplish this by selling and training the patient/caregiver online, to therapists who have their practice, through "SynPhNe Care" franchises, and community care centers.

Partner hospitals and NGOs became referral sources while being hubs of research and validation. We planned to launch this in the market in Q1 2016, after regulatory approval.

We set up a central intelligence repository to receive data online from SynPhNe devices being used in the market to deliver data analytics and visualization to patients directly. This could be routed through a therapist in a hospital, depending on the condition and needs of the patient. Therapy personalization is also automated using this data. It empowers the patient families to become independent to decide when to do therapy -- at home, at work, or while traveling on holiday.

SynPhNe markets the comprehensive solution as a recurring monthly subscription model.

We have been featured in Gizmag, Crunch Wear, Science Daily, European Commission newsletter EURAXESS, Channel News Asia, The Strait Times (Singapore), Stroke Network the USA, and other publications.

In 2014, SynPhNe received the SPRING Technology Commercialization Grant award in Singapore. In 2016, we received its first letter of intent for a case-controlled pilot study at Harvard Medical School. This strengthens our case as a technology for mainstream treatments of non-communicable disorders and disabilities.

From 2016 onwards, SynPhNe Pte. Ltd., Singapore targeted the multi-billion-dollar stroke and cerebral palsy disability market which has a worldwide manpower and technology shortage. Every year, 5 million people are left disabled and incidence levels are growing. The average annual spending per patient ranges from $12,000 to $100,000. Our initial target markets, Singapore, India, and the USA, account for an existing population of more than 10 million patients.

New Beta Product Architecture

The wearable arm gear and head gear mounted on a wireless charging dock acquires, amplifies, and transmits eight channels of brain and eight channels of muscle data simultaneously for real-time feedforward and feedback. The snap-on arm and headgear can be worn and removed quickly with two fingers. Reports using our novel metrics can are sent to the therapist for follow-up using an inbuilt GSM capability. SynPhNe puts effective stroke therapy "in a box" for use at home without the need for an existing internet or Wi-Fi network. This solves a massive global health need.

SynPhNe reported significant results from patients who began the SynPhNe training as soon as seven days following a stroke. No adverse reactions have been reported after over 600 hours of patient testing across all stroke categories.

Obstacles

The challenges and obstacles followed one another at different stages of the invention process.

Initially, the challenge was to conceptualize a "learning mode," where both brain and muscles are trained, not separately (as in current practice) but as ONE system. Next, the challenge is to decide what should be measured for clinical validation, since such a method was being implemented for the first time. During my Ph.D. evaluation, I faced the objection that our technology was "too simple" and did not have enough "engineering complexity." I argued the main complexity was in the learning model backend software; integrating body and mind. My Ph.D. was finally accepted when the clinical results showed completely plateaued patients showed up to 70 percent improvement in four weeks.

Commercially available systems for measuring electrical activity in the muscle and brain were extremely expensive, bulky, and difficult to set up for use. This was overcome by designing every sensor system from scratch, aimed at low-cost build, wearability, and "anytime-anywhere" use.

In conventional therapy, we noticed a general perception that a relaxation-focused protocol would show little or no results, and that effort on the part of the patient was paramount. High intensity using high repetitions were watchwords. Neurorehabilitation and physical therapy are two distinct fields of practice. It was difficult to convince them why it was necessary to train the brain and muscle as ONE system, using our "dynamic relaxation" method. Some of this resistance and skepticism were overcome by making the therapists wear the system themselves. This resulted in them having stress-induced imbalances, which could be self-corrected quickly using SynPhNe. The rest was progressively overcome as we gathered more data, and through patients showing obvious improvements. We were fortunate to get the support, mentorship, and advice of Dr. Paolo Bonato, Director at Spaulding Rehabilitation Centre, Harvard Medical School.

Funding has been a major challenge. The initial research work was completed with money from three competitive research grants in Singapore. During this time, both founders contributed their own money in market-related efforts, manpower support, travel, etc., which were outside the scope of the grants. They could not be delayed. We raised money from friends and family, first in 2011 and again in 2014. In keeping with our objectives of creating an affordable product, we have limited the total cost of development, validation, and patenting so far to $1.5 million over seven years.

While venture capitalists and angel investors appreciate disruptive technology, they seem uncomfortable about models which disrupt existing revenue and distribution channels at the same time. Unfortunately, real disruptive technology ends up disrupting everything. We are now engaging with actual distribution partners and advisors to develop a well-rounded roadmap. We want people in the villages to have access to the same healthcare resource as those who reside in the city. They will, thanks to the power of this new class of connected devices. By 2030, we have a vision of "A SynPhNe in every house." The first line of low-cost, home, community-based prevention, and intervention tool also treats non-communicable chronic diseases, such as hypertension, stroke, brain injury, and progression of aging.

My Inventing Advice

Having an attitude of "wanting to innovate" or "wanting to invent" is enough. Look around you and try to identify a burning social, political or environmental problem that needs a new, more effective, globally scalable solution. Or perhaps an existing poor solution (e.g., bottled drinking water) adds to the initial problem and needs remedy. Perhaps there is even an already existing, manual solution to a global problem that requires a technology concept and architecture for establishing scalability. This will align your efforts with the market from day one. Do not limit your solution to your discipline of study; think inter-disciplinary. Be solution-focused, not academic discipline-focused.

Take a serious look at the possible cost of your solution right at the start. It usually makes for a more efficient solution. Create your minimum viable product first and establish an early proof-of-concept in actual conditions rather than just simulation.

Discuss filing a provisional patent early. Never overstate your position and be conservative with what you claim. Stay engaged with those who criticize you but are fundamentally well-meaning and experts in their field. Ask them directly what will satisfy them and strategize accordingly. We did this persistently with business advisors under the SMART grant. On the other hand, do not hesitate to argue and fight with so-called experts when needed.

Look for a practical solution, not complexity. Maintain focus on those people who will benefit from your technology or process, rather than on the technology or process itself. The best technology is not necessarily the most effective. For example, the walking stick is still the highest-selling rehabilitation aid in the world.

Always allow people to participate in your invention journey. Look for potential team members who can make up for the skills and competencies you lack.

What has made the biggest difference?

To put it simply, PEOPLE. To bring any worthwhile, life-changing solution to the market which can impact hundreds of millions of people, the diversity of skills, passion, and stamina needed are mind-boggling. It cannot be the work of one or two people. Support, as well as criticism from academics, clinicians, end-users, grant agencies, and venture capitalists, are important. Fierce opposition is something that indicates you are really onto something different. It is then up to the team to question, build evidence and create acceptance then formulate a business model to create excitement in the market. Support from the families of all those involved in the project is also paramount. My gratitude goes out to key team members, advisors, business mentors, incubation partners, catalysts, agencies, patients, therapists, scientists, academicians, craftsmen, technicians, manufacturers, software developers, yoga gurus, tai chi masters, friends, and, in some cases, strangers who pitched in to help for no clear reason, except that they were good people who wanted this product to reach those who need it the most.

I must also humbly mention the support of the universe. At just the right times, the right people with the right resources appeared to help take the project to its next stage.

Lastly, I mention the "Never give up" attitude of the team. Learn from failure then try patiently and consistently without ever trying so hard that you burn out physically, emotionally, or financially. This balancing act will ensure a happy journey.

For more information and scientific publications on the SynPhNe system, please visit www.synphne.org

The Workblade - a Posture-Correct Workstation

By JC Beauchamp

Designed for all-day comfort and energy

The STANZ Workblade began as many inventions begin – out of a basic need or 'pain' that cries out for a solution. Progressively, as ergonomics matures as a science, more emphasis is being placed on workplace wellness and productivity. We are realizing just how much our sedentary workplace habits are killing us (never mind how much they are costing employers). I'm talking about the dangers of prolonged sitting and how we have become sitting ducks in our chairs.

For me, the penny dropped in 2010 when, as a college professor, I started to track the negative effects that prolonged sitting was having on my students. I noted that student concentration and motivation tended to falter during the late afternoon classes, especially with students who had been sitting through lectures for a good part of their day. As a result, I would coax my groups to stand up and stretch before I began my lecture. During discussion time, I would encourage them to walk around the classroom, the way peripatetic philosophers long ago wandered along garden paths while exchanging ideas.

My theory at the time remains the same today. Inactivity is the culprit. Getting people to move about, to shift their weight regularly, and generally keep moving, is the key to better health, greater stamina, and higher mental acuity. This is why a sedentary lifestyle is so dangerous. It simply flatlines the system. They even have a name for it now: 'sitting disease.'

A year later, I was crossing from Vancouver to Victoria on one of those wonderful BC ferries, when I wandered into the bow section of the ship. The wall under the bridge slopes gently backward. I pressed my back against it while taking in the view. At that moment, I realized just how comfortable leaning can be. People do it all the time. Lean against walls, columns, and windows, you name it, but most of the time the structure we lean against is fully vertical. I reasoned that if a device could be made with a lean already incorporated, it might prove to be a comfortable alternative to standing.

The idea of an upright workstation was born. W would develop a device with a backward lean that allowed people to get off their chairs, stay active, work upright, and feel energized by the end of the day.

I built a prototype out of a simple plywood triangle that let me adjust the lean angle, for the best combination of comfort and efficiency. I enlisted friends and family to test it after raising each work surface to match the individual's elbow heights. People reacted positively to the 'feel' of it, which encouraged me to get on to SketchUp to develop a proper design. The result was an elegant, angled pedestal with an adjustable backrest. No frills, no extras. Simply the most comfortable way to work from an upright position. I call it the Workblade, lean and mean.

I began working with a local welder who had the skills and patience to deliver three slightly different working prototypes for public trials. My job was to learn to make the backrests and for one version, with the help of a kind brother-in-law, craft a wooden frame and accompanying elevated worktable.

Once I was happy with the initial working prototypes, I registered my design and concept with the United States Patent and Trademark Office for commercial protection.

I introduced wood and aluminum Workblade options to the public in June 2012 at the Makers Faire in Vancouver. This venue draws more than 4,000 visitors annually. It was an instant hit, with CTV news coverage and lots of attention. People found the concept new and exciting.

I discontinued the wooden version to focus on two basic designs; the Highrise model made for rugged, everyday office use, and the Electra for the home market, which is easily disassembled and stored. The Workblade is manufactured locally, not in an Asian factory, so the price reflects it. In an era where many happily pay $100 for a pair of yoga pants, $500 for a decent, life-threatening chair, my customers are not just buying a product; they are signing on to the combination wellness and stamina lifestyle.

I would like to partner with a well-known, furniture or fitness brand, who can help sell my invention on a much bigger scale utilizing larger distribution and promotional networks. I believe every company concerned with workplace wellness should have these available for their employees. My company, Ergostanz, has shown there is a market for the Workblade, and I am excited for the future of this product.

SimiWeave™ is Far More than a Semi Success

By Simi Belo

I invented the SimiWeave™ because I desperately needed it!

Even though I had been plaiting and weaving my hair for many years, I was on a constant search for new ways to style and maintain it. You see, I needed something I could use to maintain my hair at home. It had to be quick and easy to use, while not damaging my hair and scalp. Most importantly, it had to look real! I loved the look that could be achieved from traditional weaves but was fed up with all the time, effort, and money involved: the headaches and itchiness, and the damage to my scalp and hair. I didn't like wigs because, as far as I was concerned, you can spot a wig a mile away! Relaxing my hair was not an option; it still hadn't fully recovered from the last time I used such chemicals in 1998.

Also, I had accepted a long time ago that I no longer had the time nor patience to sit still and have intricate extensions put in, like single plaits or twists.

I needed something that would combine the speed and convenience of a wig but delivered the realism of a weave or intricate extensions, so I came up with the SimiWeave™ design. Many homemade prototypes, compliments, and years later, I took that HUGE plunge and brought my invention to market. It was an instant success and the thanks, praises, compliments, support, and encouragement have been pouring in every day since then from people all over the world!

Your feedback is welcome, including any complaints or suggestions that will allow me to improve our products and services. I use my experience, expertise, and position to enable and empower women like myself across the world. Email me at Simi@SimiWeave.com. Don't be shy and anonymous: I can't get back to you unless you provide your correct email address. I look forward to hearing from you.

More information about the SimiWeave™ and where it can be purchased can be found at www.simiweave.com

Eric Borgos and the AdoptMe Plush Toys Update

By Eric Borgos

In 2001, I created a virtual pet site at AdoptMe.com, where kids could adopt free virtual pets

(dogs, cats, horses, fish, etc.) to learn the responsibilities of pet ownership by feeding, walking, and taking care of their pets. It quickly became popular, with around 10,000 visitors per day, of which 2,000 were new members. Unfortunately, I had zero revenue from it because my website was designed using Flash, and there was not much space for ads on it. Back then, there were fewer choices when it came to installing ads onto a website.

My idea was to make money selling AdoptMe stuffed animals (they now call them 'plush toys') in toy stores, where they would look just like the virtual pet the user adopted. They could play with the same pet both online and offline. The toy box would have an ID code on it the buyer could enter on the AdoptMe website to adopt the virtual version of the pet they purchased. Unfortunately, at the time I was overloaded just running websites and had little interest in conducting any non-virtual business.

I mentioned my idea to the person who set up my California office (the place I had never been to and have never met any employees) who thought I was crazy for not trying to do more with AdoptMe.com. So, he offered to set up a partnership to handle my toy part of the business. I had nothing to lose since I would never do it myself, so I agreed.

To make a long story short, it did not go well. We were able to get some plush toys manufactured in China and began selling them at AdoptMe.com. I am unable to remember the exact figures, but our cost was around $2 per animal and we sold them for $14.95. We sold around one unit per day, which was fine. But our goal was to sell them in lots of stores. We had some sales in local stores and eventually, after much negotiation, we were able to convince Toys "R" Us to test our AdoptMe plush toys. Originally, they were going to test in 60 stores, unfortunately, they only tested it in their Times Square, New York store. This was one of their busiest stores, so it was a great place to test. The AdoptMe toys ended up selling fairly well, considering we hadn't promoted them, other than advertising on our website. But, for Toys "R" Us to continue selling our product, it has to be a huge hit, which it was not.

We could have tried selling our toy in other stores, but three years had passed without making much money. Our product liability insurance for the toy costs $800/month. In addition, the cost of an employee and office suite, etc., so we decided to dissolve our partnership.

Today, Webkinz is doing the same thing we did and making millions of dollars doing it. Perhaps we were ahead of our time. I still own AdoptMe.com, which is doing well, and overall, I am happy. I had given the toy business a try, even though it did not end up making money.

Update

In the end, it had cost me around $40,000 extra to create the AdoptMe Toys business. I wound up putting my money into the partnership over the three years just to keep our project going. Some of this money went to improving Adoptme.com, so at least that was beneficial. My partner also put money into it. In the end, he wanted to sell or liquidate AdoptMe Toys (including the website) to help recover some of his money. I did not want to sell the website, so I gave him $25,000 to fully own the website.

A few months later, the employee who had been working for us offered to purchase the website and toy business from me for $125,000 but needed three months to get investors. He had moved to China, and since virtual pets were a hot item there, it would be easier to find a good manufacturer. Unfortunately, he was unable to raise the money. While I was waiting, I modified Adoptme.com, allowing it to have better ad space on it, and the revenue shot up from $300/month to $3,000/month. So, I was happy to keep the website.

The website made good money for the next few years, but eventually, the income declined to a few hundred dollars a month to about $50/month. The main problem is the website is programmed using Flash and Flash is dying. Many mobile devices, including all iPhones and iPads, can't play Flash, so no one is building Flash websites anymore. It would be much too expensive for me to convert the site to another format, so I am letting it die a slow death. It had a good run while it lasted.

Attorney-Inventor's Idea Is Making a Gentle Splash

By Sandra Bretting

Baby care seat's concept originated in the shower, became a reality on vacation

More than 30 years ago, Melanie Spratt-Anderson found herself caring for her two infant siblings More than 30 years ago, Melanie Spratt-Anderson found herself caring for her two infant siblings while she was attending junior high school, since her mother worked two jobs.

"My routine in the morning was that my mother would get in the shower and then I'd pass her first one baby, then the other. That was the best way to do it," Spratt-Anderson said. "I believed there was an easier way."

Over the next three decades, Melanie would earn an economics degree from Texas A&M and a law degree from Southern Methodist University.

She practiced family law for five years, then was elected county prosecutor in West Texas.

A turning point in Jamaica

Through it all, Melanie continued to sketch ideas for her invention: an infant seat that parents could mount in the shower. She wanted it to be high enough so parents wouldn't need to bend over and be sturdy enough to hold a baby up to 18 months old.

"Think about it," said Spratt-Anderson, now 45. "I had an idea that involved both an infant product that's used in the bathroom. As far as liability insurers or anyone else was concerned, I might as well have been selling the most dangerous thing – like a piece of glass to newborns."

The turning point for Melanie's idea occurred in late 2011. She had taken a vacation to Jamaica, where she met Omar Graham, a local welder, who'd recently become a fitness instructor. He offered to create a prototype for her in exchange for free legal advice.

The result, in February 2012, was the first iteration of Wash That Baby.

"It looked nothing like the product does today," Spratt-Anderson said. "He used scrap metal, so it was very boxy and very heavy. It weighed at least 10 pounds. Her eventual design is called Wash That Baby. Today, Wash That Baby is a 4.5-pound foldable seat made of PVC-coated nylon with aluminum bars for support.

To develop the product, Spratt-Anderson and Omar Graham, her Jamaican partner, secured assistance from the Jamaican Business

Development Center. The center loaned them engineers and product designers to refine her baby seat in exchange for a modest fee. Over the next year, the team modified the design until they believed their product was ready to be certified by a laboratory that contracts with the Consumer Product Safety Commission.

"Passing this test became a nightmare," Spratt-Anderson said, "It would take working through seven additional prototypes before they were able to pass this test." By her estimate, Melanie has spent $20,000 to get her invention refined to its current state.

Success at the trade show

In October 2014, Melanie was invited to show it at the ABC Kids Expo in Las Vegas, Nevada. It's the country's largest trade show for baby, child, and teen products.

"We had about 50 applications for only 18 spots," said Judi Sunden, an account manager with the ABC Kids Expo. "We call it the Invention Connection, and it allows inventors to get out there in the public, to see if manufacturers are interested, and determine if there's a market for their product."

Following the ABC Kids Expo, online retailer Amazon began offering Wash That Baby with a price tag of $100.34 in February 2015.

Editor's Note: We would like to thank Sandra Bretting, Eric Kayne, and the Houston Chronicle for allowing us to reprint this article. We asked Melanie the following two questions:

What were some obstacles and how did you overcome

them?

The two biggest hurdles I had to deal with were defending my product in the patent application and figuring out the required Consumer Product Safety testing needed for this unique product.

In the Patent process, you have to look at similar products and persuade the patent officials that your product is different and better than previous patents granted. In my patent research, I found there were baby seats and shower seats, but no baby shower seats. The arguments and claims took some creativity by me and my patent attorney from Legal Zoom in writing our patent application.

Navigating the Federal Safety Rules for US products was also very confusing. I'm an attorney and I had to re-read the regulations 100 times to understand!

What advice would you give to those interested in inventing?

Don't get discouraged by the obstacles. If it were easy, everyone would do it. It took Henry Ford 10 years to invent the car. Having a great idea is just the beginning. Be prepared to persevere in developing your invention, then manufacturing, marketing, before ultimately selling them. It took the inventor of "wheels on a suitcase" a year to get any store to show interest in his product!

Also, read/listen to stories of other inventors for inspiration and motivation.

Acid Reflux Patient Finds Relief & Starts an Online Business

By Adele Camens

It all started in 2000, with a scratchy throat and laryngitis

I assumed I was getting a cold, so I took a decongestant and drank hot tea. It didn't work. My throat got worse and my voice almost disappeared. After a week of self-medicating and getting nowhere, it was time to call my internist. I was sure it was strep throat. He would prescribe an antibiotic, and I would be cured. Instead, after a negative strep test, he sent me straight to an ear, nose, and throat doctor. I got scared.

A GERD Diagnosis was Good News

At that point, I was a 17-year breast cancer survivor and a five-year ovarian cancer survivor. My antennae went up, along with my anxiety.

I just wanted to have strep throat. After some tests, the ENT doctor said, "No problems here, you have acid reflux." Impossible, I assured him. I rarely have heartburn or those other symptoms. He ignored my MDL degree (doctor of motherly learning) and directed me to a gastroenterologist. Yes, I had GERD (gastroesophageal reflux disease). "Your esophagus and throat are being irritated at night by the acid coming up. Take this prescription and sleep elevated on a wedge pillow." Fine, I replied, where do I get the pillow? His answer? "I don't know." I started the medication and started researching on the Internet.

Mild Acid Reflux can be Controlled by Gravity!

After several days of research, I learned that every authority recommended the same solutions: a) sleep with your head elevated 6 to 8 inches, b) make sure your entire upper torso is supported on an angle, and c) avoid certain foods. With no chocolate to calm my nerves (good for the girl, bad for the GERD), it was time to enlist the help of our younger son, then a radiology resident. He sent me to a few obscure medical websites where they confirmed the research conclusion: The simple answer appeared to be gravity!

It was so logical. Acid reflux happens when a muscle at the base of the esophagus, the lower esophageal sphincter, relaxes. Instead of preventing acid from coming back up the esophagus as it should, it allows acid to "reflux" or go back up, causing irritation. If the acid were kept down, the irritation would lessen and not be a problem. Methodically, I began the hunt for a wedge pillow.

I felt like Goldilocks. This one was too uncomfortable, too inconvenient, too expensive, but mostly, they were all too short. Due to the lower esophageal sphincter muscle being located at the base of the breastbone, you need to be supported throughout your entire torso. So, 24 inches wouldn't be long enough. I wouldn't want to disturb my husband by elevating our bed on blocks. Have you tried putting pillows between the mattress and box spring on your side of the bed only? I did. All it accomplished was making our bed lopsided.

Knowing What to Buy was Easy — Finding It was Difficult

I knew what I needed. I just couldn't find it: a foam triangle, 6 to 8 inches high at the top and at least 30 inches long. I was at my wit's end. My husband solved my problem with a simple suggestion: call our neighbor who designs and manufactures pillows.

Right away he agreed. It seems like many people had asked if he made an acid reflux pillow and now, he could say, "Yes." We discussed dimensions and came up with just the right size and shape. It worked! After several nights of sleeping on my MedSlant wedge, I felt much better. Of course, the medicine also helped, but it was expensive. I would prefer a lifestyle change rather than take medicine.

I stopped taking the medicine, but after a week my symptoms reappeared. I resumed taking the medicine while continuing to sleep using my wedge. After three weeks of using my pillow, while avoiding acid-producing foods, I was able to stop taking the medication. Eleven years later, my symptoms have not returned.

Meantime, we had given wedge pillows to a friend with acid reflux and her husband who suffers from sleep apnea. Both were helped. We improved our washable, poly/cotton cover, rippled the foam for added comfort and coolness. We were ready for testing and evaluations by volunteers. Friends referred friends; my gastroenterologist gave them to patients, and we were on our way. When I took some forms to the printer, the girl who helped me asked hopefully, "I have a horrible time with acid reflux. Could I please try it?" A week later she called to tell me it worked great and requested another pillow! Her manager was pregnant and suffering from acid reflux. I learned from my gynecologist that pregnancy-related reflux can practically be eliminated by sleeping on a wedge. A pediatrician who had an infant and a two-year-old suffered from acid reflux. We gave her two pillows. She reported back they had helped her tremendously.

Our MedSlant Wedge Pillow Was a Hit!

We had more than 80 pillows tested to rave reviews, but there was one more wrinkle to be ironed out. When I traveled with my husband for his clothing business, without my pillow for 3 to 4 nights, my symptoms would reappear. I tried taking it along, rolling up the pillow with rubber bands. Nothing worked. So, we decided to make it fold. We tried Velcro, glue, and fabric strips. The pillow still didn't fold. Finally, we fashioned a fabric hinge cover for two pieces of foam that would allow them to fold yet still act as one piece when open. Perfect! We now had a pillow that would provide a drug-free, nighttime relief. We added a zippered, handled, travel bag for go-anywhere convenience. With our United States patent in our pocket, we built our website.

An Online Business was Born

People began emailing and calling us to tell us how it had helped. They referred their friends and told their doctors, who recommended

MedSlant to their patients. My research had shown that sleeping on a wedge had other benefits too; reduced or eliminated snoring, relief from nasal congestion, and asthma symptoms. It's easier breathing for heart patients. My family is feeling much better. My husband no longer snores, so we both sleep better. Our granddaughter has asthma. Sleeping on our pillow allows her to breathe more easily. She no longer wakes up with puffy eyes. Our kids use them when they have colds. Our daughter found it so comfortable she sleeps on it regularly, just for the fun of it. Of course, the wedge pillow is not a cure-all. Some of the diseases and conditions it helps, while others require medical advice and medication.

The Simple Solution is often the Best

We tried embellishing our product, using memory foam and other bells and whistles, but the only difference it made seem to be adding to the cost. We made one valued improvement. Each piece of foam is encased in a zippered, easily removable, washable cover. My husband reminded me of that business adage...KISS– Keep It Simple, Stupid. It takes gravity to keep acid down and your airway open. We've invented a product that is simple and affordable, that works. I am grateful that, through my struggle, I am now able to help others improve the quality of their lives. Enjoy it in good health!

For more information, please visit www.medslant.com

Spray Away Cleaner & Stain Remover

By Beth Chester

Spray Away Cleaner & Stain Remover is a non-toxic germ, mold, and mildew-killing EVERYTHING cleaner

It is a stain-removing, laundry detergent and carpet shampoo booster, fabric softener, wrinkle releaser, hand sanitizer, and deodorizer all-in-one. It dissolves brake dust and bloodstains on contact. Spray Away eliminates blood, coffee, red wine, and pet stains without harming the color, fabric, or material. It cleans, disinfects, and removes stains from everything -- all in less than 10 minutes!

My Invention Story

I'd saved up enough money to replace my carpet in my colonial-style home after spilling an entire cup of coffee on the carpet in my bedroom. I tried cleaning the stain using my Electrolux Carpet Shampooer, then a Bissell Carpet Shampooer and Extractor, and several other stain removers. Nothing worked.

Returning from the carpet store, having chosen the carpet to be installed, I found my cat unresponsive on the floor. He needed life-saving surgery that was going to cost the amount of money I had saved for it. I chose to save my cat's life. With the holiday season approaching and wanting my home to look immaculate during them, I needed to find a cost-saving solution.

So, I went into my kitchen and began testing ingredients I hoped would work. I had taken chemistry in college and believed I would either burn a hole in my carpet, take the color out, or clean it. As I poured my ingredients into the mixture, a chemical reaction took place. I felt if it burned a hole in my carpet, it would be an improvement anyway. So, I sprayed it onto the coffee stain next to my bed in front of my 25-year-old daughter. The coffee stain began to vanish before our eyes. I was so glad she was there to witness it.

We both were completely shocked by what was transpiring. We allowed it to air dry and found the stain had been completely removed. Most importantly, it had not harmed the color or the carpet. It felt soft to the touch and smelled fantastic. We felt compelled to use it on all of the carpeting and the upholstery with amazing results.

I sent it to a few labs and companies, such as Proctor & Gamble and Johnson & Johnson. A lead chemist at one of the labs emailed me before I finished sending samples to labs and companies. He said, "Come on, Beth. We have chemists here that have doctrines in chemistry. Don't you think we would have thought of this by now?"

"No," I replied, "because nothing works like this." He advised me to file a patent before sending the formula to him or anyone else. He has since become a mentor. He tested my formula against Tilex, Mr. Clean, OxiClean, Windex, and more. The results were found to be superior.

At this point, I hoped to sell my formula. I shared these findings in the business community to gauge interest. I said it works on everything better than anything selling on the market. I had proof of outstanding results. Satisfied customers were calling it "the best thing since sliced bread." I made sure everyone knew it was non-toxic and killed germs on contact.

I was visiting the emergency room of my local hospital when I noticed its floors (amongst other things) were filthy. I took pictures and sent them to the facilities manager who passed them on to the man in charge of housekeeping. He had earned his Ph.D. in Chemistry and had invented SepTek, a chemical that is used to break down the waste found in septic systems. He ran a swab over a desk that looked clean. Then inserted the swab into a machine that produced a score.

Next, he sprayed the same spot with Spray Away Cleaner & Stain Remover and wiped it clean. He shared with me his opinion that non-toxic cleaners do not kill germs. I began to sweat. He swabbed it, then inserted the swab into the same machine. The machine lit up and his mouth dropped open in amazement. He also has been become a mentor of mine. This energized me.

I had previously taken a college course in entrepreneurship, where we learned about business, how to create a business plan, etc. I remember learning how important it was to thoroughly understand your business. I have been a professional athletic instructor and a restaurant manager. I used to own a gym but had to close it due to members not being able to afford the fees.

I let them use it for free, even paying for several of them to participate in the National Cheerleading and Dance Competitions at Disneyworld. I started a non-profit organization attempting to raise money, but my community did not think of cheer and dancing as a charity they wanted to support. It nearly killed me to close my gym. I never imagined in a million years I would sell anything, especially a cleaning formula.

Could I compete with huge companies with massive marketing budgets, who have been selling their household cleaners for years? I had doubts that I could earn a living selling my cleaner. I would move forward, and glad that I have.

My sales have doubled every year. I'm not where I would like to be yet in terms of sales. I've had several laboratories test my cleaner who've shared with me their results. Unfortunately, the findings are not strong enough for me to be able to make these claims on National Television or Worldwide yet. That's where I am focused on next. I met with a buyer for QVC's and the Home Shopping Network. He liked that my cleaner works so well on so many things, especially that it's non-toxic. I have begun manufacturing it in the United Kingdom, having performed an in-depth market analysis, with encouraging results. I have auditioned for ABC's Shark Tank.

I need to have a laboratory, certified by the Consumer Product Safety Commission (CPSC) test my product and declare it safe for public use. Their report needs to verify that my formula kills germs, and what the germ-killing ratio is. My hope is they certify it works better than OxiClean and Shouts in removing stains, and better than OxiClean in laundry detergent boosting power. This will cost at least $30,000.

I have been approved for a Small Business Administration (SBA) loan. However, I will need to generate a lot of sales just to be able to pay it all back. I believe this to be possible by obtaining national exposure. I've applied for a grant in the Chase Drove Grant Program for small businesses and have people willing to invest their own money. I may need to go that route to have the testing done. However, I will cross that bridge when I come to it. I've joined Business Networking International (BNI), where I met the man who is helping me start our manufacturing process in the UK. He is currently testing its market for viability.

I found it to be extremely expensive to try to obtain a US patent and worth my time pursuing. I had attempted to patent my Spray Away Cleaner, but the patent office declined to award me. The reasoning is anyone can make a cleaner in their kitchen, therefore no longer issuing patents for cleaners. I learned that if granted, my ingredients would become public knowledge, so anyone can steal my formula. I have another patent that I have been perusing. It's been pending for 2 years; far, too long in my opinion. I have spent more than $20,000 on them so far.

My advice is to listen to your gut. Be honest and upfront about everything you do. Believe in yourself, even when no one else does including your spouse and siblings. Give back when you can and try to make a positive difference in the world.

To view videos of my product in action, making some of the toughest stains vanish before your eyes, please visit our Spray Away Cleaner

Facebook page or the Beth Chester Channel on YouTube.com. To

purchase some or to download more readable information, comment, or contact us, please visit www.SprayAwayCleaner.com

Tyga-Box Systems

By Nadine Cino & Marty Spindel

We Are Tyga!!

We are the spirit of innovation, the essence of elegant design, the stewards of sustainability, and masters of efficiency. We're compelled by efficiency because efficiency compels markets.

Tyga-Box was a love child — unplanned!! We got everything we deserved for having hired the low-price rogue mover some 20 years ago, well before municipal recycling was available.

Nadine — being half-Cuban, half-Italian, and all Latin — burst into a rant saying, "Why doesn't somebody have a business that rents reusable plastic boxes as an ecological alternative to corrugated?" Marty – being half-calm, half-reflective, and all Jewish – said, "If you'd just listen to yourself, you have a good idea."

You couldn't find two people who knew less about the moving industry than us. At that time, Nadine was successfully expanding her international fashion design consultancy. Meanwhile, Marty was enjoying his 17-year career at a prestigious Manhattan law firm, is highly regarded for his talent in the esoteric fields of trust and estates and philanthropic grantmaking.

Our inexperience turned out to be an advantage

We started the business by renting a "stand-alone" plastic box. In our desire to attract customers, we met them on move jobs so we could learn something about this new, disruptive business we had just launched.

We noticed that the process of packing a corrugated box and putting it on a dolly was done as two separate steps. We observed that people often strained to lift heavy boxes after packing them. Movers needed a great deal of time to distribute dollies throughout an office, then load corrugated boxes onto them – one box at a time. Since corrugated boxes are generally too weak to be stacked higher than three, it would typically take two dolly loads to hold the entire contents of a single file cabinet.

Our "aha" moment came when, peering into the truck at origin, we saw the greatest inefficiency of all! As dolly-loads were rolled onto trucks in stacks of three corrugated boxes each, they only consumed about three feet of height, while trucks have eight feet of height available. About 5/8 of the truck was being used to move air!

We realized that one small change in the packing process would make one big change in the moving process. The key was to "pack the box while aboard the dolly." That would eliminate both the lifting of heavy boxes and the distribution and loading of dollies. And, if the boxes were made from strong plastic, they could be stacked high enough to both hold the contents of an entire file cabinet in a single stack and utilize 40 percent more of the space inside the truck.

Those factors struck us as much-needed gains in safety and efficiency. On top of that, reusable plastic boxes (with a life of over 20 years) would bring some much-needed gains in eco-friendliness over single-use corrugated boxes.

Unintentional inventors of the non-tip bottomless dolly

To "pack direct to dolly," the dolly had to be delivered at the same time as the box so that it would be on hand at the time of packing. For that, we needed a "low theft appeal dolly," so that it would not be stolen while waiting to be packed.

That insight led us to become innovative and unintentional inventors to design the worlds' first-ever non-tip bottomless dolly which transformed the way weight was supported from a horizontal plane to a vertical one, essentially suspending the weight of the boxes placed upon it. We integrated the fit between box and dolly with a tongue and groove interlock, and finalized the engineering of our innovation, known today as the "Tyga-Box System."

We gathered up almost every penny we had in the world and laid it down as a deposit to have molds made. Marty withdrew the entirety of 17 years of contributions to his pension and profit-sharing plan at the law firm and Nadine mortgaged her five-family Brooklyn home to the hilt.

As we had once chosen a rogue mover, we chose a rogue mold maker

What became obvious was how little we knew about mold makers and mold making or to be present to the cliche: "the road to hell is paved with good intentions." As we had once chosen a rogue mover, we chose a rogue mold maker. A well-intentioned one-man machine shop, housed in little more than a garage in Deer Park, Long Island, he took our money and made molds that failed!! For the second time, we were on the verge of bankruptcy!

We spent much of our little remaining cash for Nadine to take a flight to a fashion industry trade show, where she hoped to find new customers. In the last place, you would expect it – the classified section at the back of an in-flight magazine — Nadine came upon a tiny, half-inch ad by a mold maker in the Midwest who was not only offering to build molds but finance them over the cost of production. Running between flights at an airport, Nadine stopped at a phone booth, called Marty, and breathlessly shouted, "Call this mold maker!" Days later, Marty was on a flight to meet him.

No more "one-man machine shop." This was a "real" mold-making company with a big factory and a large staff of professional engineers on board. We finally got it right. The owner of the company was intrigued by our vision for an "integrated box and dolly system for office moving" and he agreed to finance most of the cost of the molds. Nadine's dad gave her the deposit, her inheritance which he wanted her to have while he was alive so he could see how things turned out. We were underway – again!!

AT&T gave us our first order — a rental of 8,000 Tyga-Boxes

While the molds were being made, Nadine kept designing fashions to bring in money and Marty kept renting our inventory of stand-alone plastic boxes. Then, one day, Nadine and Marty joined together, on a sales call to AT&T in New Jersey. Their Lucent Technology division was moving to a new location, and they wanted to be the first company to use our new "Tyga-Box System." They gave us our first order – which was for a rental of 8,000 Tyga-Boxes – for a product that had never been field-tested before!

The molds were completed and the first production of Tyga-Boxes came off the press just in time to fulfill the AT&T order. We both personally participated in rolling the first delivery of empty stacks of Tyga-Boxes off our trucks and into Lucent Technology offices. We both watched in breathless amazement as the first Tyga-Boxes were packed and stacked by Lucent employees. We held each other's hand tightly, as the first stacks of Tyga-Boxes and Tyga-Dollies were rolled out of the origin building and onto trucks bound for their destination.

And the promise of our "aha" moment came to fruition, when, peering once again into the truck at origin, we saw the greatest efficiency of all! Tyga-Boxes uniformly stacked five-high, filling 40 percent more of the capacity of each truck, and reducing the total number of truckloads by 40 percent!

Metrics — reduced AT&T's cost of moving from $209,000 to $143,000

The move was a total success. And AT&T wrote us a letter of recommendation, citing that the Tyga-Box System had not only made the move easier, safer, and more efficient, but had reduced their cost of moving from $209,000 to $143,000, or by 32 percent%!

Shortly after that, we moved into a "real" office in Midtown Manhattan; we rented a "real" warehouse in Long Island City and filled it with Tyga-Boxes. We hired our first real employee to manage our office. Nadine closed shop on her fashion design studio and the two of us set out on a year-long series of two-week road trips. From city to city, across the U.S.A, we did "dog and pony" shows of our new Tyga-Box System to any company that would listen. We'd spend two weeks on the road and then two weeks back at our office, closing deals and setting up appointments for our next road trip. By the end of that year, the Tyga-Box System was being used by companies moving and moving companies throughout the United States.

Other companies copied us and brought knock-offs to market

As is the case for many successful inventions, other companies that would copy our integrated box and dolly concept soon cropped up and brought knock-offs to market that designed around our patent. But even when we see competitive products in the market today – and sometimes bristle — we also feel gratified that our original concept was good enough to be copied and Tyga-Box remains the absolute safest, most cost-effective moving system available nationwide.

We are awed by the realization of the power of a "napkin-sketch idea," unsuspectingly borne from a Latina rant, to invent a solution to a problem that has been hiding in plain sight for decades. That realization transformed both our lives and the way that office moving is done throughout America.

Sometimes, we like to think that, perhaps, somewhere, we have seen a tree that wouldn't be there if not for Tyga-Box.

Since its inception, we have generated one trillion Tyga-Box reuses, reduced carbon footprint by 150,000 tons, eliminated 400,000 tons of cardboard from clogging landfills, and saved 20 million trees from being destroyed. Those trees provide the air supply to 40 million adult Americans every year.

For more information, please visit www.tygabox.com

Michael and Ernest Falcon and PLUNGER-in-a-BAG

By Michael and Ernest Falcon

What inspired us to invent the PLUNGER-in-a-BAG Toilet Plunger?

Over the past five years, I have unclogged countless toilets, especially as my wife and I were teaching my young daughter how much toilet paper to use before flushing. Invariably, after hearing a shout-out to "FIX THE TOILET," I would make the trek across the house from our utility closet, where we hide our plunger, to my daughter's bathroom. After unstopping the toilet, I would then have to carefully tip-toe back to the closet with a plunger in hand, hoping that it would not drip on our carpets, thus creating an additional mess.

During one of my parent's visits to our home, my father asked whether we had a plunger and a garbage bag so that he could unstop the guestroom toilet. Curiously, I asked why he needed the plastic bag, and he said, matter-of-factly, that he was planning to place the wet plunger into the bag afterward so that it wouldn't drip on our carpets when he returned it.

Immediately, the proverbial light bulb went on; that's the solution to my nagging plunger dripping problem! From then on, I have always transported and stored our plunger in a plastic bag. When a toilet becomes clogged, I unstop the toilet and then place the plunger into a bag to prevent drippage on our carpets while transporting it and to eliminate puddles on the closet floor while storing it.

After that eureka moment, my father and I developed prototypes of a plunger with a built-in bag dispenser for quick, easy access to leak-proof bags and filed two patents. As the applications worked their way through the patent office, we were hopeful that our invention would be useful to others.

Confidence in our product increased when I stayed overnight in a hotel and had to contact housekeeping to unclog my hotel room toilet. To my surprise, housekeeping arrived carrying a toilet plunger in a plastic garbage bag, and I immediately understood that it would be a public relations nightmare for the hotel if guests ever saw housekeeping walking down the hallway with a dirty, wet plunger, dripping all over the hotel carpets.

Finally, we became determined to bring our product to market last year when we noticed several new toilet plungers designed with a carrying canister or "caddy" being sold at local retail and hardware stores. With some of these bulky, awkward plungers selling for more than $15, we knew that our simple, intuitive product could be manufactured at a much lower cost and could succeed in the marketplace.

Trongs - Keep Your Fingers Clean

By Dan Ferrara

While working late one night in early 2008, my business partner, Eric Zimmermann, and I decided to take a break and grab some buffalo wings.

We were having a conversation about whether it is easier to invent something or market it then convince people to change for the better. Just as we began eating, my cell phone rang and I scrambled to wipe his fingers clean. Not able to do so quickly enough, I missed the call. At that moment, we realized the obvious utensil that the world had been missing, and the concept of the Trongs was born. Right there at the table, we began sketching ideas on a napkin, and so our journey began.

For the next year, we worked to create dozens of different models of this new utensil, continually improving the design. We generated CAD models of each new version then had prototypes made via 3D printing to test the design. It was a long, expensive, and tedious process, but we knew that for this product to work, it would have to be both comfortable and effective.

Once the design work was done and we were satisfied with the functionality of the model (#12), we began our search for a plastics injection mold toolmaker. We found one we liked in Indiana and hired them to build our first, four-cavity aluminum injection mold. About two months later, Eric and I flew to visit the facility in Indiana to witness the very first mass production of the Trongs utensil.

Knowing that we would be in Indiana, we set up a meeting with the Director of Marketing of a locally based chicken wing chain restaurant. We brought the newly made Trongs with us to the meeting and he loved them. He invited us to come back two days later for the official opening party for that location and told us the president of the chain would be there. At the party, we met with the president and a few other executives from the company and they agreed to test Trongs in one of their locations, intending to expand to all of their restaurants if the test went well. Eric and I couldn't believe it was that easy! We quickly learned that our instincts were correct. It seemed too good to be true... and it was.

We planned a return trip to Indiana later that month to launch Trongs and it was all uphill from there. On the day we arrived, they had a major snowstorm in Indiana, so business was much slower than usual. On top of that, the product we were supposed to have delivered to the restaurant didn't make it there in time. Our manufacturer was unable to produce the Trongs as quickly as he assured us, he could. We made some calls and located another manufacturer based in Kentucky, who was willing to drive to Indiana in the snowstorm to pick up our mold, bring it back to his facility, and start making Trongs to be delivered the next day.

We were excited about the launch and we got to the restaurant early the next morning. We found that the owner of that location was testing Trongs in his restaurant, but he was doing this at the request of his corporate superiors. He saw Trongs as an unnecessary expense for his business and therefore, he wasn't assisting us in promoting the product. The wait staff was just dropping Trongs on the tables with no explanation of what they were, so customers weren't using them. We knew that this feedback to the executives of the company would not be favorable, so we attempted to contact the Director of Marketing to let him know what had gone on. We were surprised to find out that the company had restructured and he was no longer in that position. No one else would return our calls.

We decided to work with some independently owned restaurants in the New York area, where we live, to do some test marketing. We found that some people instantly got it and appreciated the benefits of using Trongs. However, many didn't like the idea and said things like, "I like getting my fingers messy. That's the fun of eating wings." We also saw some flaws in the design, which caused some new users to fail on their first attempt and not want to try Trongs again.

Eric and I spent the next few years testing and modifying the product, creating a new design that would be more comfortable, and address some of the issues we had in the past. However, at that point, we were deeper in debt with no free cash. Other things got in the way. We were both working our regular full-time jobs throughout this process and working on Trongs at night and weekends. In October 2010, my wife gave birth to my son, which forced us to put Trongs on hold for a while. We continued to sell retail packs via our website, but we weren't actively pursuing and new sales channels.

Then, one morning in May 2012, my cousin emailed me to suggest that I submit Trongs for review by producers of Invention USA on the History Channel. I had watched the show before but had never considered submitting Trongs, so I sent them an e-mail. About a week later, we received a call from Invention USA, letting us know that we had been chosen for the show. They flew us out to California to film a segment on the show and as a result, we were introduced to a VP at Sonoco Plastics, who agreed to become our new manufacturer.

The fire was re-ignited for us and Eric and I was in full Trongs focus mode once again. We had a 60-second infomercial that had been on our website for years. We decided to shorten it to 40 seconds and re-posted it to YouTube. As a result of this minor change to the video, blogs and websites began posting it and it went viral with more than 280,000 views in just two days (now more than 400,000 views). The Invention USA show hadn't aired yet and we were seeing a huge spike in sales due to this new publicity.

Eric and I were excited about the airing of Invention USA in November 2012, but we still didn't have the money to build the new mold with the modifications we had made. At the end of October 2012, I decided to go all in, and I took a loan against my 401K to pay for the new mold so we would be able to begin production for the sales that were bound to come once the show aired.

On Nov. 26th, 2012, our episode aired and the sales started rolling in. Since then, we have been exploring many new retail sales channels (daily-deal websites, TV sales, retail chain sales, etc.) to raise the capital to build a much larger eight-cavity, steel mold to be able to handle the volume needed to sell wholesale to restaurants. So far, retail sales have been going well and we have grown out of shipping from my living room. We now have a fulfillment company that stores our inventory and ships our orders. The increasing popularity of smartphones and touchscreen tablets has assisted in the acceptance of this new utensil. The need to stay connected has overpowered the desire to resist change.

Our company is still growing and we aren't rolling in dough yet, but we are well on our way to our ultimate goal of having Trongs in every wings and barbecue restaurant.

We never could have done it without the help we received from our family and friends throughout the process. No more mess!

For more information, please visit www.trongs.com

The PerfectSeal™ Gets the Stamp of Approval

By Mike Forehand

In 1988, a customer contacted my company to purchase three electric embossers

There was only one brand available at the time, and I had no experience with the unit at all. I did some research with users and dealers and found this brand of electric seal was undependable. I should have known when the manufacturer said it had just decreased the warranty to 60 days from purchase. The customer was going to purchase these units no matter what my advice.

In the next sixty days, I made five repair trips and had no support from the manufacturer. The customer and I became very frustrated at such a poor-quality product. My wife said: "why don't you just build your own?" I think she was just sick of hearing me complain, but she was right!

Being familiar with the mechanics of this brand of electric seal, I felt I knew what not to do, so I began a three-year endeavor. I consulted seal users, design engineers, and product manufacturers, then studied design criteria, calculated force, and drew more sketches than I had ever done before in my life. I was spending money with machinists for test samples, just to throw them in the dumpster due to a design flaw.

The criteria were easy: (1) a seal impression from a touch-of-a-button, (2) extended life of electric models over handheld models, and (3) no chance for repetitive stress injury. Sounds simple, doesn't it? In 1991, after 14 designs and about 100 variables, one simple design worked. When I made the very first test impression, my first word was "perfect." That was the basis for the name PerfectSeal™. The simple design with only two moving parts has proven durability and dependability time and time again.

In April 2005, I implemented the fifth generation of updates but still have not changed from the original design. My PerfectSeal™ heavy-duty, high-volume units produce a minimum of 200,000 high-quality impressions from just a touch of the button. These units are supported with a 60-day "final approval" time on one unit to assure each customer's total satisfaction and have an unmatched two-year or 200,000-impression performance warranty.

It is much easier to justify the cost of an excellent-performing quality product than to justify a poor-quality product to less cost. Fortunately, PerfectSeal™ is a better product for less cost. Nothing can be more aggravating than being left out in the cold if the product does not perform well or being left all alone without manufacturer support.

The final approval time on one unit allows a first-time user to be convinced or return it. If you don't like your PerfectSeal™, don't keep it! This policy was created because I am so confident of the user safety, value, and performance of PerfectSeal™, and that you will be nothing short of "impressed" with every impression.

The value of any electric embosser should be the increased durability, extended life over manual embossers, and the insurance of removing any chance of repetitive stress injury during use. Repetitive stress injury is a major concern. One claim could cost several thousand dollars and a major loss of employee time. Companies spend thousands on ergonomic products for computers, desks, tables, chairs, etc., and are looking to minimize risk and increase performance when using their seals and other marking products.

Electric seals are changing from heavy-duty high-volume users only, to include the standard duty users like notaries, tag agents, architects, schools, and small court systems at a more affordable price. PerfectSeal™ motorized is a standard duty electric embosser that operates a common die holder from an existing or new hand-held embosser. This innovative design will convert any existing manual hand-held seal to an electric operation at the lowest price ever offered. An unlimited number of hand-held seals can be converted to a "no stress" electric operation.

More information regarding Perfect Seal is available at www.southernmark.com

Abigail Forsyth and KeepCup

By Abigail Forsyth

My brother and I started a café business called Bluebag in Melbourne in 1998

As the business grew, we became increasingly concerned about the volume of packaging waste our business and our customers consumed.

We looked to purchase and sell reusable cups as an alternative to disposable but observed that not only were existing options unsuitable for specialty coffee, but they also hadn't won the hearts of consumers.

Ceramic mugs were heavy, breakable, needing to be heated before filling, and impossible to dose correctly with milk and coffee. Thermoses were bulky, unattractive and invariably the coffee shot had to be poured into the Thermos, destroying the crema on the shot. Further to this, both options were made of composite materials, making them dishwasher unfriendly and difficult to recycle at the end of life.

We had the notion to make our own but were daunted by the enormous costs of setup and manufacture. My moment of clarity came when I was heating the milk in my daughter's sippy cup one morning. Imagine if I gave her milk in a disposable cup and then discarded it? That idea seemed so wasteful, yet I did it with coffee twice a day! This moment was the call to action.

We took a huge gamble that usability and aesthetics were the key reasons for the poor take-up of reusables as an alternative to disposable cups. Our café experience was invaluable in providing input to make the KeepCup work behind the coffee machine as well as for the user.

Almost four years later, with a great deal of help from design professionals, we have kick-started a behavioral change in Melbourne that is spreading across the world. People purchase KeepCups. After all, they love the way they look and feel, and continue doing so because they form a positive habit. For many of our customers, it has been the beginning of a journey to reduce the consequences of convenience behavior. Feel good. Do good.

KeepCup is from Australia with love. The environmental footprint of our products is really important to us, so we were committed to local manufacture. Sustainability is linked to usability, and we believe; quality and underpins the ethos of the business. As the business expanded globally, we were hesitant to proclaim our Australian manufacture. However, it turns out this is a positive message and 'made in Melbourne' even more so, given our city's reputation for specialty coffee.

In 2012, we opened a warehouse in the United Kingdom, and in March 2013 we opened in Los Angeles. Local presence means that we can begin to tell a local story in these markets – stories of local assembly, local printing of packaging, and point of sale materials while reducing the environmental footprint of the KeepCups.

KeepCup also uses less plastic. Disposable cups are lined with polyethylene and have a polystyrene lid, so there is enough plastic in 28 disposable cups to make one small KeepCup. In 2009, Simon Lockrey from the Centre for Design at RMIT completed a Simapro Life Cycle Analysis, which has independently verified our sustainability claims. Research conducted by Canadian chemist, Dr. Martin Hocking found the break-even energy requirement to manufacture a reusable plastic cup versus a paper cup over a lifetime use was under 15 uses.

Since June 2009 we have sold more than three million KeepCups, diverting billions of disposable cups from landfills.

KeepCups are now sold in 32 countries around the world. We think of ourselves as a campaign supported by a product, where the best reusable is the one you use. Ours just happens to be pretty awesome.

Many small acts will make a phenomenal difference.

For more information, please visit www.keepcup.com

My Tot Clock

By Pamela Gonzalez

People often ask me how I came up with the idea for my product

My answer is easy --sleep deprivation was the mother of my invention!

It all started four years ago when my oldest son Gabriel was two years old. His new little brother Anthony arrived and took over the baby room, along with everything in it, including the sacred crib. Gabriel was a great sleeper in his crib, but when he got into his big boy bed, all bets were off. He became a master negotiator before bedtime. He required Mommy to be in the room before he would fall asleep. He would wake up in the middle of the night (sometimes multiple times) and finally end up in our bed.

This became our routine, which was 100 percent created by a Mommy who didn't have the heart or the strength to let her big boy keep crying it out. One night, or should I say the wee hours of the morning, I was putting Gabriel back to bed for the second or third time when it dawned on me that the problem wasn't that Gabriel loved waking up in the middle of the night and disturbing everyone's sleep, but that he had no idea what time it was!

So, I came up with what I thought was a great idea! I would tell Gabriel that he couldn't get out of bed until the sun woke up. Genius move, right? Well, not exactly. Gabriel woke up every hour to tell me that the sun was awake! I knew I needed something better than the sun to solve this problem! I needed to buy one of those clocks. You know, one of those clocks that change colors, so children would know when to sleep and when it's okay to get out of bed.

After putting Gabriel back down...again, I hit the Internet (hey, I was up already!), and started searching for the magic clock! I searched and searched to no avail. The clock was nowhere to be found, so I vowed that night to invent it!

Well, I got busy as we moms do, and I didn't start working on my magic color-changing clock for more than a year, although it never quite stopped gnawing at me. In the summer of 2006, I finally decided to sit down and put my thoughts on paper. Within a day or two, I had a full concept document.

After putting the concept together, the next step was to figure out what this magic color-changing clock would look like. I invited my good friend Ben Yin (graphic designer extraordinaire!) to lunch to see what he could help me come up with. He had two little girls almost the same age as my boys, so he quickly grasped the concept and we started brainstorming ideas. We agreed on a throw-back style design with a changeable faceplate and a child-friendly handle.

You can't have a concept without a name, so I decided it was time to name my baby. Here

were the top name ideas before I came up with the winner:

- Magic Color Clock
- Magic Time Machine
- Nighty-Night Clock
- Sleepy Time Clock
- Kid Klock
- Tike Time
- Tick Tock Toddler Clock
- Tick Tock Tot Clock

I started calling the concept Tick Tock Tot Clock, which sounded like a fun name, but I always worried that it was a bit of a tongue twister. Then, one night as I was settling into bed, it hit me -- My Tot Clock! I got so excited, that I jumped out of bed and wrote it down. It had all the elements I was looking for: short, catchy, rhythmic, and descriptive. I also loved the word "My" since I wanted small children to love their clock as much as they loved their favorite "my" toys.

Now what? I needed to patent it! I picked up all the patent-it-yourself books, read most of them, and decided to hire an attorney. I conducted interviews with half a dozen patent attorneys in the Dallas area and finally decided to hire a very well-respected sole practitioner named Michael Diaz.

Mike and I worked hard to complete the Provisional Patent Application, which essentially allows you to date-stamp your idea until you have the time and money to submit the much more extensive Patent Application (PA). Although I had a year to submit the real deal, I was so anxious to get things cooking that I went ahead and submitted it a few weeks later. Mike, being one of the good guys, only charged me for the PA. Thanks, Mike.

In the process of submitting the Patent Application, we also went ahead and submitted the Trademark application for My Tot Clock, which I'm happy to say, has officially been issued. The Patent Application is still in the works (two long years later).

The good news is that you don't need a patent to develop a product; you just need one to protect it. The bad news is that it doesn't take much for the copy-cats to design around your patent (or your product) if motivated to do so as I, unfortunately, learned the hard way.

At this point, I was starting to spend some serious time and money on my concept, so I decided it was time to start a company and reap the tax benefits. I thought through lots of company names and settled on White Dove Innovations as a tribute to my mother who passed away in 2004 from ALS (Lou Gehrig's Disease). I know she would have been enormously proud of her daughter for pursuing this project.

After settling on a name, I submitted my Doing Business As application, and I was in business. A couple of months later, I decided to file my company as a Limited Liability Corporation. White Dove Innovation, LLC was officially born, complete with an Employer Identification Number, a bank account, a P.O. Box, a telephone number, and business cards.

Why, do you ask, did I feel I needed a P.O. Box and a telephone number? How else was I going to get junk mail and phone solicitors? Hey, it didn't matter. I was basking in the glory of being Pamela S. Gonzalez, President of White Dove Innovations, LLC!

So, now I have a concept document, complete with a visual of my product idea AND a patent application! Now what? Did I need to SELL my idea to a company that could build and market it, right?

From everything I read, I knew the big boys were mostly out of reach, so I started researching the second and third-tier players. I prioritized the players based on the product line, distribution, and willingness to evaluate independent ideas. Then I decided to approach the first company on my list.

I submitted all the paperwork to the process owner (aka "gatekeeper") and waited, waited, and waited. I finally called to inquire about the status of my submission. She said that they were extremely backlogged and wouldn't have an opportunity to review it for nine months. Of course, being a new starry-eyed inventor, nine months seemed like a lifetime to me, so at 2 a.m. the next day (when I was putting Gabriel back to sleep...again), I sent an email to the president of the company. To my amazement, he wrote to me a couple of hours later (4 a.m.!) and said that his VP of Product Development would be in touch.

Two days later, the VP of Product Development called. We had many great chats and tons of emails over the next couple of months. He said they were extremely interested in the product idea but were in the process of a major company restructuring, so they wouldn't be able to focus on it for another six months. Well, I was a Mommy on a Mission, who had no intention of waiting six months, so I decided to build it myself.

Warning to my Online Friends: The VP of Product Development ended up going to another company and taking my idea with him, even though we had a Non-Disclosure Agreement (NDA) in place and my patent was pending. In autumn 2008, his new company launched a product that was extremely similar to My Tot Clock. I guess they thought they could design around my product and get away with it. Thankfully, they're missing a few key features, like the great bedtime stories and lullabies. They may have made the steak, but they completely overlooked the sizzle!

As part of the two-month dance with the aforementioned company, I was asked to prove that my concept would work. In my heart, I knew it would, but they wanted proof. Mommy's intuition isn't enough in the business world, so I had to build a prototype.

The very first prototype I built was made from digital timers, nightlights, and a CD clock radio. I plugged the first-timer into the blue nightlight and set the bedtime. I then plugged the second timer into the green nightlight and set the waketime. I set the alarm on the CD clock radio to the same waketime and voila! We were in business! (I also threw in a red nightlight to test the timeout concept and it worked great!)

Now that we had a real working prototype, it was time to prove the concept. My wonderful husband and I made 10 prototypes and recruited all our friends with small children to participate in our little test. We promised to serve margaritas, so it wasn't too hard to get them interested.

The next step was to run the test and document the results. We set up the prototype in our boys' room, got them ready for bed, and started the fun task of explaining to them how their new magic lights were going to work. Anthony, who had just turned two, could describe the colors and seemed to take it all in stride. Gabriel, who was almost four, quickly understood the concept but was still a little suspicious of this new contraption in his room.

When the light turned blue, we put the boys down and left the room. This was completely outside of their routine and did not make our two-year-old happy. He wanted Mommy to rock him to sleep as usual, but I stayed tough and calmly reinforced the blue light / green light concept. Big boy Gabriel was sad but brave. Anthony screamed for 40 minutes and finally fell asleep.

Although getting the boys to sleep the first night wasn't 100 percent successful, keeping them in bed was! Both boys slept in their beds the ENTIRE night without calling out even once, and that was a FIRST for our family! They were so proud and we were beyond thrilled! On the second night, Anthony cried for 15 minutes before falling asleep. Gabriel was very calm and cooperative. By the third night, they both went right to bed when the blue light turned on without so much as a peep! This became our new, wonderful sleep routine!

The proof-of-concept was a huge success. Children who had never slept in their beds were sleeping on their own within the first few nights. They were no longer waking up in the middle of the night or too early in the morning. They weren't negotiating. They were waking up better rested and so were their parents. We were definitely on to something!

Now, we needed to figure out how big the market was. We started by searching for existing research (known as secondary research), and we found plenty. Our favorite statistics included:

- Juvenile Products Annual Sales: $7.1 Billion

- Annual Market Growth: 8%

- # of U.S. Children Ages 2 – 5: 16 Million

- # of U.S. Babies Born Each Year: 4 Million

- # of Licensed U.S. Child Care Centers and Pre-K Programs: 180,544

We then decided to conduct our survey (primary research) to understand just how many toddlers (ages two to five) experienced various sleep issues. We set up an online survey using SurveyMonkey (www.surveymonkey.com) called "The 60-Second Toddler Sleep Survey." Within two weeks, we collected nearly 300 responses from people throughout the country! Here is what we learned:

Toddler Sleep Study Statistics (Ages two to five)

- 70% of Toddlers Negotiate Before Going to Sleep

- 35% of Toddlers Sleep with Their Parents Part of the Night

- 20% of Toddlers Sleep with Their Parents All Night

- 50% of Toddlers Wake Up in the Middle of the Night
- 40% of Toddlers Wake Too Early on Weekdays
- 60% of Toddlers Wake Too Early on Weekends

We were thrilled with what we learned through our research and decided it was promising enough to continue the journey.

Now that we have proven the concept and gathered promising market research, it was time to hire an engineer who could create something a little more marketable than my contraption of nightlights and timers. After an Internet search and several interviews later, I hired Innoquest, a design/engineering/manufacturing firm out of Woodstock, Illinois (www.innoquestinc.com).

I knew when I talked to the president of Innoquest, Bill Hughes, that I had my guy. He asked all the right questions, immediately identified some possible challenges, and just had a way about him that I liked. He became my right-hand for the next several months and continues to be a trusted advisor today.

Within a couple of months, not only did Innoquest come up with the technical design for My Tot Clock, but they also developed 20 prototypes for use in our field studies and tradeshows. I can't begin to explain the excitement I felt when I pulled the first working prototype out of the box. All I could think was, "Wow, these little puppies are going to be sitting on store shelves one day!" I was practically floating.

Then, I put one of the prototypes in my boys' room. They had been using their nightlights and timer contraption for five months now and were deserving of the real deal. They loved everything about their new Tot

Clock: the lights, the story, the music, the handle, everything. Their reaction was more than I could have hoped for. I was overjoyed!

A great big Thank You to Bill and the Innoquest team.

Once we had working prototypes, we decided to test the real market. In April 2007, we headed to none other than the Juvenile Products Manufacturing Association tradeshow in Orlando, Florida. We wanted to find out if the industry would welcome our product with open arms. To our delight, we picked up more than 100 business cards from chain buyers, store owners, catalogs, e-tailers, and sales reps, all of whom were interested in knowing more about My Tot Clock.

My husband and I had a fantastic time at the tradeshow and the results were exactly what the doctor ordered to keep us energized as we continued the journey. Now was it being time to get serious and find a manufacturer. I had been interviewing manufacturers for a couple of months by the time we hit the trade show and was down to a short-list of two. To my excitement, there were two exhibitors at the tradeshow that were actual customers of the manufacturers on my short-list.

When the show started winding down, I decided to take a little break to visit the exhibitors. I waited for a good time to introduce myself and let them know that I was in the process of interviewing their manufacturers. I asked if they had a few minutes to discuss their experience with these companies. They were more than happy to tell me everything I wanted to know and then some. To my excitement, both exhibitors provided A-plus recommendations on the two manufacturers. What a blessing to have met these exhibitors. Now I had peace of mind knowing that both manufacturers were upstanding companies and good partners to their customers. Now it was time to focus on the deal!

After nearly two months of back-and-forth with the manufacturers, I finally received detailed quotes for the non-recurring costs (engineering, programming, and tooling) and the production costs of the product. They were within 10 percent of each other...and 50 percent higher than I hoped. I decided to bring in a third manufacturer to validate the cost estimates and, wouldn't you know it, they were also right in line with the first two quotes. I had to reset my expectations.

I finally decided on Innovation Design Products (IDP) as the manufacturer for My Tot Clock. Their quote was competitive, but what made them stand out was their work ethic throughout the entire sales cycle. They worked hard to prove to me that they were capable of building my product. They worked through most of the big issues during the sales cycle and already had solutions. I also appreciated that their quotes were detailed and easy to understand. I felt like I knew what I was getting with this company.

We signed a deal and got started. I was assigned to project manager Ringo Ling from Hong Kong. Ringo and his team of engineers, programmers, quality assurance specialists, etc., have done a tremendous job as we have built My Tot Clock together.

At nearly 15 months, the development of My Tot Clock was a test in patience and perseverance. In my naïve thinking, I was convinced we could produce My Tot Clock in six months easily. Well, product development is never easy, and there is always a bump or two in the road. For us, there were a few more than that.

Lights

Our first challenge was with the lights. We had to come up with a cost-effective way to illuminate the various lights uniformly across the full surface of the clock. The IDP engineers found a great material that would capture and distribute the lights evenly, and we were able to print the clock right on it.

Syncing

Our next challenge was to find a way to keep the digital clock and the analog clock in sync. Although it would have been much simpler to exclude the analog clock completely (and use color only) or implement an analog-like digital clock in the front (which isn't child-friendly), I stuck to my guns until we found a solution. My engineers worked together (Bill Hughes and IDP) to come up with a way for the digital clock to send a volt pulse to the analog clock motor at the top of each hour. Voila, we had synchronization.

Programming

This was by far the most time-consuming task of all. We spent months programming, testing, re-programming, and re-testing until we got it exactly right. All the functions operate beautifully together, just like clockwork.

Tot Clock Treasures

Although the programming took the longest amount of time, it was the Tot Clock Treasures that nearly did me in. In my naïve thinking (again!), I was convinced we could implement an MP3 solution and play bedtime stories, lullabies, and wake songs of any size and length we desired.

Although I wanted to start with child-friendly cartridges, I also planned to set the product up for future digital downloads. It was going to be great! But, that kind of greatness comes at a great big price and would have easily priced My Tot Clock out of the market and I simply couldn't let that happen.

My engineers worked through this issue diligently until they found a 32MB chipset that would allow us to deliver an eight-minute bedtime story, lullabies, white noise, and an awake song for the right price. Now our challenge was to get all the content small enough to fit on the chip.

Now that we had the right chip, we had to find the right content to put on it. I went through my children's CD collection and found that most of their music was produced by Twin Sisters Productions (www.twinsisters.com), so, I called them. Why not start at the very top, right?

I was able to speak to one of the sisters right away, Karen Hildebrand. She was a super nice lady, very professional, and excited about my product. We agreed on a licensing deal for her music and bedtime stories and we were in business.

I also found a wonderful bedtime story called Welcome to Children's Dreamland by writer/illustrator Ashley Paris. The minute I heard it, I smiled and thought what a perfect story for My Tot Clock. It's filled with positive, loving messages read in a slow, almost hypnotic way. I loved it and so did my little testers!

Unfortunately, the dozens of fabulous bedtime stories, beautiful lullabies, and fun wake songs were too big to fit on our 32MB chip. I needed to find an industry expert to down-sample the content, and I found them right in my backyard!

The Dallas Audio Post Group (www.dallasaudiopost.com) is a leader in sound engineering, not only in toys, but also in film, television, and radio. Roy Machado, the founder, explained all the limitations of the chipset. He then came up with an approach to deliver the best possible results and worked directly with the manufacturer to make it happen.

Thanks to Twin Sisters Production, Ashley Paris, The Dallas Audio Post Group, and IDP, we were producing seven fabulous Tot Clock Treasures as part of the launch. Children are going to love picking their favorite bedtime story and plugging it in all by themselves. Say goodbye to night-time negotiations!

As you can see, I have had many business partners throughout this journey, but through it all there has been one constant (other than my husband of course!), and that is my Art Director, Joe Potter (www.joepotter.com).

I found Joe through Elance, which is a must-use service for any entrepreneur that connects buyers with service providers via the internet. Of all the freelance graphic designers I spoke to, Joe was the only one who had experience with all areas I was seeking (website, marketing materials, product labels, packaging design, logos, and more).

From Day 1, Joe did not disappoint! Not only has his work been top-notch, but he is truly one of the nicest people I have ever met. Even when we're on draft 20 of a deliverable, he always keeps his positive, upbeat attitude. Thank you for all you do, Joe.

For Joe to finalize all his deliverables, he needed lots and lots of pictures. Before the trade show, I had hired a local commercial photographer to take a few shots of the early prototype. The cost was a whopping $500 for two shots! Unfortunately, I didn't have the luxury of time, so I paid the money and made a note to myself to find a cheaper photographer.

When I received the first factory sample, I hired Upgraded Images (www.upgradedimages.com). Ken Greenlee did a fantastic job, every bit as good as the original photographer for less than $20 a shot. I also had to hire a photographer to take shots of children sleeping, waking, etc. for the website and packaging. I found a local photographer named Dan Walters (www.applecreekphoto.com). The minute I met him, I knew he would be great with children, so I hired him. Just as suspected, Dan had the patience of a saint and somehow managed to get some great shots of three highly active tots.

If you're wondering who developed our fabulous website, it was Cratima Interactive (www.cratima.com) out of Bucharest, Romania. Like Joe Potter, I found Cratima on Elance (now rebranded as Upwork), and I am so very thankful I did. They have been wonderful to work with -- fast, professional, highly skilled, and extremely focused on customer satisfaction. My project manager, Alina Lupu, has kept everything moving forward, even when I started to run out of steam.

On Dec. 8, 2008, the first six units off the assembly line were inspected and the factory was released for production.

It has now been two years since I started working on My Tot Clock, and we were finally ready to launch! Oh happy, blessed day!

We hope you will be amongst the first to give your family the gift of better sleep through a fun, innovative, child-inspired product. A great big, loving thank you to my wonderful husband, or as he calls himself, the Vice President of Stuff (VPS) for White Dove Innovations. He has been my rock, my support, and my sanity throughout this journey and has selflessly picked up the pieces at home while I pursued my dream.

Thank you to my dear family and friends for the constant encouragement and support. Not once did they tell me I was crazy. Thank you to my precious children, Gabriel and Anthony, for being such horrible little sleepers and the inspiration for My Tot Clock.

Thank you to all the wonderful focus group mothers and the cute little testers.

Thank you to my mentors and dear friends Todd Price and Jon Feld for all their wonderful guidance.

Thank you to all my online mentors at www.inventored.org who have been a tremendous source of learning and inspiration.

And of course, thank you to God for laying out the path, giving me a little push, and lighting every step of the way. Thank you to all my partners who helped me bring this product to market.

More information about My Tot Clock and where to purchase it can be found at www.mytotclock.com

Why are People So into this RootSuit Thing?

By Colin Grussing

A lot of people buy RootSuits because they love our story of entrepreneurship, determination, and fun

We hope you like it.

The Backdrop

In 2008, I had just graduated from college and was looking for something to devote my time and energy to. I had watched my friends give up on their dreams of living a life busting at the seams with fun, passion, and joy in favor of real jobs. I've always been determined to find the fun in all things.

After a few odd jobs here and there to make ends meet, I saw one of these weird green spandex bodysuits on TV and thought that my friend would enjoy wearing one. I searched and searched but couldn't find a single company that sold them online—so I decided to start one from the ground up with the help of three close friends: Brandon, Hampton, and Victoria. We sourced, designed, and manufactured the suits, after a significant process of trial and error and a serious learning experience.

First Jumpsuits Arrive

The first suits off the production line were way beyond our expectations. We couldn't wait until Halloween; we had to put them on right away. We got so amped that we ended up in the French Quarter, where the crowd went so wild for the outfits (think free shots, unsolicited kisses, and hundreds of go-get-em-Tiger butt slaps); we knew we were on to something.

Our First Sale

I put the first one up on eBay to see if anyone would buy it, and it ended up selling for

$400. (I refunded all but the normal price—because the buyer seemed like a good guy and it seemed unfair) At that point, I coded my first website to try selling this type of full-body jumpsuit. They went like hotcakes! My friends and I had no idea this would be the response we would get, and we were so happy. This was just about a month before Halloween, and there was no way we could keep up with demand.

By early October, all 2,500 had been reserved and there were 2,500 more people on a waiting list. We tried extremely hard to get more suits.

I sent a friend to China on Oct. 29 to pick up 400 more. He stayed for 18 hours and flew back. Somehow, he made it through customs. We found a customer willing to put him up and they shipped 400 suits in one day out of the guy's dorm room. It was craziness.

After Halloween, customers started requesting all sorts of products, and we tried to cater to every request. We went from producing and selling one color to 15 colors then expanded into patterns such as flags, animal prints, and ninja suits. While we've experimented with a lot of types of stretchy products at this point, we think that what we have now represents the stuff you guys like the most, though we're happy to always hear our loyal fans' suggestions.

New Website

Our second website launched in early 2008 so customers could easily choose from our large selection of colors and products. We refocused our company, experimenting with many types of spandex and zippers, making sure that our suits were of the highest quality and wouldn't break when we wore them outside and got rough with them. Selling high-quality products was sincerely important to us—and we were only happy when we thought we had the highest quality product that we could make.

Phone Calls and Emails

Since the beginning of RootSuit, we've always believed that our customers are everything, and we've tried to provide the best customer service that we possibly can. Our phone number has been posted at the tip-top of our website so that people can call us and ask us questions or just shoot the breeze about how much fun they're having in their suits. In just a short time, we went from getting hundreds of emails and calls per month to thousands. But they started coming in so fast that we couldn't answer them all. We had to take shifts and hire more friends to help us take care of all of our customers. It was a blast! Our team of four friends could talk about nothing else other than RootSuit, sharing the antics we were hearing about what people were doing in the suits.

Ha, the Antics

As we started to sell more spandex suits, the customers thank-you letters, pictures, and videos started rolling in. Our customers were doing everything from streaking across baseball fields to partying, bungee jumping and even skydiving (please don't do this with the mask up, please, please). We wanted to commemorate some of these special moments with blog entries and allow customers to add their memories. Our Facebook page exploded with volume and activity, and we couldn't have been happier.

Exposure

It was about this time in 2010 when a couple of really significant exposures of people in spandex clothing came out. The green men in Vancouver, supporting the Vancouver Canucks, got some serious media attention for distracting hockey players in the penalty box. Shaquille O'Neal also chose to wear an XXXXXL RootSuit while hosting an awards show.

Since the exposure, and our success, we've watched numerous copycats and low-quality competitors pop up, and grow the exposure to this product, especially in Europe. It's amazing to think of ourselves as a global brand that's been in business for almost five years now, but the market has gotten tougher for RootSuit. We're excited to grow, but we've always kept a careful eye on quality, tempering our interest in producing more suits with our ability to get them to our customers on time and make them the best quality that we can.

The Future

RootSuit is a pretty mature and stable business now, so I've gotten to do what love most: start new businesses. The new hot costume this year will be the Workaholics Bear Coat. This will be another extremely fun business. Once the rush dies down, I look forward to wearing bear coats out and doing more fun events and photoshoots. Earlier this year, I also started a business selling motorcycle sidecars. They are so much fun. I swear they will be getting much more popular in the next few years.

In 2014, we launched a venture called 52 Businesses where we started a new business every week of the year, documenting the adventures in a blog and podcast. It should be very entertaining and educational. The goal is to promote entrepreneurship by pulling back the curtain and demonstrating the accessibility of the skills and resources needed.

For more information, please visit www.rootsuit.com

The Socket Saver™

By Jessica Haynes and Barry Connelly

Sometimes you wake up with a good idea

My husband, Barry Connelly, had this experience. We had the annoying household problem of loose wall sockets and appliance plugs falling out while vacuuming, drying our hair, blending foods, or turning on reading lamps. Not to mention Barry's electric garage tools stopped working while in use when the plug fell out of the wall. I said to him, "I'm tired of holding my hand next to the plugs to keep them from falling out."

He was a former service station owner and auto mechanic, so he knew a lot about how to replace worn-out sockets. But the process involved buying new wall sockets, turning off the electricity to each circuit with a bad plug, re-wiring each new receptacle, then turning everything back on. And, of course, resetting the clocks in each affected room. With so many loose wall sockets, he kept putting it off.

Our invention journey began when Barry came up with a smart and effective solution. He woke up one morning and said, "I have an idea." In the garage, he created a crude prototype out of a small plastic child safety device made to prevent children from shocks from electrical outlets, using a file, knife, and sandpaper, and it worked perfectly. The loose wall sockets were like new again in seconds. I was happy that this problem was solved. It was safe and easy to use.

The first step - getting a patent

It became clear that we needed a good patent attorney. I had a client in Ohio who was considered one of the best in the field and I called him about our idea. He liked it and started the process. He said to tell no one and we signed a letter of confidentiality.

We sent our patent attorney a refined prototype and our patent went through easily. There was nothing like it on the market. No competition. Our attorney was surprised and pleased for us.

The next step was to get a mold made to produce the Socket Saver for the public. The bids were expensive for a plastic polypropylene mold, as high as $15,000 for a single cavity mold as opposed to $5,500 for the same quality. We kept researching. Barry found a local plastic molding company that liked the idea, was reputable and our manufacturing agreement began. The quality was excellent! The final product looked great and worked perfectly. Our lesson was to keep looking for the best company at the best price, with the best reputation.

Inventor Challenges

In the beginning, we approached a number of the big companies that could benefit from our invention. We received several responses from the legal departments. They each sent us a lengthy 30-page contract asking us to waive our rights to the invention and patents. They wanted the invention, just not to pay for it. Our patent attorney said, "No." So, we waited and looked for better options.

A local friend introduced us to Don Varner who invented the California Water Blade. His huge success with Costco and other major outlets was exciting. With Varner, Barry came up with the idea of the Socket Saver Wall Plate. So, we were on to our second patent. (Simply replace a worn-out receptacle wall plate with the Socket Saver Wall Plate and your loose wall socket problem is fixed in seconds). Now, consumers had two great options: a Socket Saver that can go anywhere with you and a designer wall plate that solved the problem.

Our second patent for the wall plate had some challenges. Our patent attorney had retired and we needed to find a new resource.

A new firm was highly recommended. We ended up spending thousands of dollars with lots of unexplained bills. But this story has a silver lining. I met one of the best patent attorneys in my life. She said, "Jessica, follow me to my new firm." We did. Within a few months, our full utility patent was issued. This covered the wall plate and the original Socket Saver. Now we were doubly protected. And she didn't charge us for the filing fees and other processing expenses to make up for how much she believed in the product and how much money we were overcharged by her previous employers.

Our Expanding Market

We started getting more and more orders and positive feedback about our invention through the internet. We had a wide appeal to renters, homeowners, college students, B & B's, RV enthusiasts, and business owners with older buildings. We also found a market with travelers who encountered loose wall sockets at airports, and motels, and who could not charge their cell phones, laptops, and other electronic devices because the plug kept falling out. The Socket Saver proved to be a huge Christmas stocking stuffer success as an affordable and desirable gift.

Early on, I secured SocketSaver.com. With sales, we secured the trademark for Socket Saver. Also, we secured our next utility patent, for the use, method, and kit of the Socket Saver. SocketSaver.com attracted customers all over the country.

Working Out of Our Home

We had every order shipped out the next day. With Barry's business background, he set up a system through the website and our webmaster to receive orders, collect the payment, and ship the product. It was seamless and our customers were happy with the Socket Saver, the cost, ordering online, and our timeliness in delivery. Ten Socket Savers sell for $9.99.

With my marketing background, I created several videos in a professional film studio. They came out very well. Some are funny, some are to the point like, "As Seen on TV", and some are informational. You can see them on the website and YouTube.

Through the videos and the websites, we were invited by Invention Home to the Las Vegas Hardware Trade Show. It's the largest trade show of its kind in the United States and features some 2,600 booths, featuring well-known brands and new products throughout the U.S.,

China, and Mexico. We met numerous new and experienced inventors and learned so much about packaging, marketing, promoting, and connecting with buyers.

Making Key Connections

Besides the invention itself, I had another trump card. I met Barbara Bigford, the inventor of The Beach Pocket. Her invention keeps your beach umbrellas from blowing over at the sea or lakeshore. Millions of Beach Pockets have been sold around the world, and Barbara is in demand as a speaker at colleges and universities. We met through my consulting business and became fast friends.

She has been a wonderful advisor. Her experience of coming up with an idea and getting it to market success has been a genuine treasure. She notes that the statistics of an invention making it is three percent. Luckily, we have made excellent connections that believe in us and we have a fantastic product. Today the Socket Saver ™ is a popular product in ACE Hardware and TRUE VALUE stores.

Getting to this point of success involved trial and error and learning what to do and what not to do. We have these additional suggestions to share about coming up with an idea and turning it into a successful company:

Write it Down

When you have an idea, write it down ... when you thought of it and date it. Get a patent-pending document so your idea is registered and won't go to someone else who is thinking of the same idea. We have heard so many stories from people that had a great idea but didn't follow through immediately and lost their chance for ownership.

Packaging

We needed a package that stood out and got the message out to customers in seconds. We hired a professional package designer. He suggested a design for clip strips and pegs to get the attention of customers as they walk through the aisles and as a front of the store, impulse-buy purchase. (The clip strip visual is highly effective for new products.)

Media Coverage

Print media is often the best because a person can read the article and save it, putting it next to their computer, or telephone or hanging it on the refrigerator. We called the local newspapers and shared why our invention was big news. With this coverage, readers went to stores and asked for the Socket Saver ™, and demand was created.

Presentation Counts

For the stores, we wrote what you would call an elevator speech or a sales sheet that explained the product in a few sentences along with customer base, demographics, and wholesale/retail costs so that we could create an ongoing program that was beneficial for the retailer and us. One sales sheet included satisfied customer comments from our website and Amazon.com, and another specifically about the Socket Saver ™ and the benefits for sales in the corporate market.

Trade Shows

Go to a trade show to see how the professionals are selling their products and learn how to market your invention. You will learn so much as a new inventor. We often call this "University 101." Collect business cards. Likely you are meeting people just like you that are manufacturing. Since we knew the trade shows we could talk intelligently to the buyers of the corporate market.

Keep Calling Your Contacts

Getting into ACE Hardware was a process. Through a friend who had ACE contacts, we were given an email address to the NorCal ACE buyer. It took 10 calls and follow-up to finally hear him say, "Let's make this work!" and we were in the door. The General Manager has worked for ACE in the capacity of buyer for 35 years and sees 5,000 new inventions every year. By not giving up and having a product that matched their market an alliance was created.

Shark Tank

If we received $1 for every person who suggested we get on the television show Shark Tank, we would be rolling in money. But we chose to do it ourselves and it has proven to be a good move. Now when we talk with the corporate leaders, the fact that we 100 percent privately own our company, they are more interested. Also, the Socket Saver ™ is made in the USA. This continues to be valuable to customers and retailers.

Making A Difference

Along our journey, we have had many nay-sayers who said we would never succeed, and roadblocks, including attorneys who took advantage of us. Yet we always pulled through. The internet was a major factor. With our website SocketSaver.com and sales on Amazon.com, we built a solid record of sales that the Corporate Market liked.

Customer Reviews

I wish I'd known about customer reviews years ago. Here are some comments:

- About half the outlets in our house are very loose. Plugs fall out of them. (We have even tried using some packaging tape to hold a few of them against the wall, but that never worked). Works great, Will order more.

- These are awesome! House built in the 1940s and these make a huge difference for everything we plug in.

- Works like a dream! I had a very heavy night light that was slipping out of my outlet. Put one of these in and it has been working perfectly for over a month! Super happy!

- These little gadgets are amazing! My hairdryer plug no longer falls out of the socket every minute.

- These things are awesome for anyone who has loose plugs and doesn't want to replace them. (Renting) thanks, they work great!

- I love my Socket Savers ™! Great for my home and I now travel with them... I wish I would have thought of the idea.

- Great for my parents' home. Many of the outlets are 65 years old dating from the time of construction and it's hard to keep things plugged in. Not anymore. This adapter fits over the existing plug and stays very well when plugged in.

- I was having issues with many of my sockets and was thinking of replacing many of them. I am so glad I found the Socket Saver ™. I did not replace any of my sockets. I use the socket Savers ™ with many of my appliances. I am so glad I found this product. They are perfect.

First, I'm overjoyed that this works. You slide this plastic piece over your current device's outlet prongs and that's it. You're done. It takes one second. And it works perfectly. It's almost humorous how simple it is and how it works.

Light Phones

By Joe Hollier & Kaiwei Tang

If how we spend our days is "always connected," always staring at our screens, that will be how we spend the rest of our lives

Our ability to be fully present at the moment is diminishing quickly as our constant desire to document and share has distanced us from experiencing our lives as they occur.

We might say that we have talked to someone when we have not. We have texted, emailed, snapchatted, tweeted, posted, commented, or "liked" them. We often connect in these ways while in the presence of others and thus are not fully present when conversing with them either.

Everything is moving us towards more connectedness, fighting for more of our attention and more of our increasingly limited time. These products are engineered in ways that use our vulnerabilities against us.

Multitasking is a myth. It is addictive and exhausting. It is glorified procrastination. We've become habitually overwhelmed and we are craving escape.

Why is the same giant computer phone that you bring to work the same phone that you bring to the beach, to dinner, to bed, or when simply trying to enjoy an afternoon away from email? There are times where you don't need a computer in your pocket, where'd you be much happier without one. A carpenter does not use just one tool. A carpenter uses the right tool for the job.

The Light Phone is your second phone. It is designed to make the experience of "going light" special. It removes the barriers between us and the real people and real things we love and care about right in front of us.

We met inside of Google's inaugural incubator and quickly realized that the last thing the world needs is another app. In a world where we are capable of building just about anything, it's even more important than ever to consider what it is that we want. We're interested in the very personal relationship that we have with technology, from the moment we wake up and first interact with it in the morning until we go to sleep at night. It should respect, encourage, and empower you to be your best. Technology has the potential to be great, and we're here to bring a little bit of humanity back into the equation.

Joe is an artist and Kai is a product designer. Joe has worked doing everything from film, photography, and stop-animation to collage, illustration, and running a skateboarding company. Kai has 10 years of experience in product design development, and as a project lead, he has traveled around the world to bring 12 mobile phones to life.

We are not able to do this alone, we have a great team of people helping us make the Light Phone a reality. Our hardware team is made up of four engineers that have worked with Kai on phone projects in the past and cover all the areas of expertise. Wolfrey, Alans, and Henry are located in China, while Matt is in Taiwan. They are working daily to oversee our manufacturing partner.

Our software team, David, Kyle, and John, are located in Seattle. They handle our cloud platform, the app, and the dialer software on the Light Phone itself. Light is headquartered in New York City, which is where Kai, Joe, and our great team of advisers are located.

We are still a small team embarking on the endeavor of bringing a mobile phone to life. Something that we realized after launching our Kickstarter campaign was just how little we as consumers understand about the process of manufacturing technology. Even making a phone as simple as ours requires enormous supply chains with thousands of people involved.

We want to share the story of bringing the Light Phone to life in the hopes of becoming more conscious consumers together. Understanding the process that goes into the objects that make our lives so privileged gives us a genuine appreciation for the things we own, and hopefully not a constant yearning for more.

Find out more at www.thelightphone.com

The Macy Catheter

By Hospi Corporation

The Macy Catheter was invented by Brad Macy, a veteran hospice nurse and recipient of 2013's National Hospice and Palliative Care Nurse of the Year Award

The inspiration for its invention came directly from a memorable patient interaction.

Over the years, Brad has seen thousands of difficult symptom management cases while assisting patients and their families in the middle of the night. The most challenging cases were when the patient could not swallow medication and end-of-life symptoms were spiraling out of control.

One night, Brad had a patient who was experiencing severe terminal agitation. The patient was shouting, climbing out of bed, and was very frightened and suffering. Brad got orders to administer a sedative to assist in calming the patient. As the patient was unable to swallow, the prescribed route of administration was via his rectum. He administered the sedative in tablet form rectally as prescribed and waited "that difficult wait" for the patient to calm while giving the patient's son emotional support.

An hour later the patient was worse. The wish of both the patient and family was that he be able to die peacefully and at home. Brad called the doctor again for a repeat dose of sedative. When preparing to administer, the second dose he realized the previous dose was still undissolved in the patient's rectum.

Brad was left with a dilemma that is well known by every experienced hospice nurse: how to help a patient who is experiencing severe symptoms and unable to swallow reach a state of comfort within the home setting.

Motivated to reduce the severe agitation and suffering of his dying patient, Brad found a way to give the medication as a suspension that would absorb quickly in the patient's dry rectum. He crushed the tablet, added water, and administered the medication suspension into the rectum with a urinary catheter. The patient calmed down quickly and was sound asleep within 30 minutes. The patient's son was deeply grateful for an easy solution that controlled his father's symptoms with minimal subsequent discomfort or disruption. The patient died peacefully at home a few days later.

Given the successful outcome of this case, Brad decided to create an optimized device to facilitate this intervention. He subsequently co-founded Hospi intending to make a commercial device available that could provide comfort and relief for patients and their loved ones on a much larger scale than would be possible as a lone practitioner.

Hospi developed the Macy Catheter to improve the patient and caregiver experience with a serious or terminal illness. It is designed to maintain patient comfort and dignity while leveraging the speed and established benefits of rectal administration. The Macy Catheter is of particular relevance during the end of life when it can help patients to remain comfortable in their homes. It can also reduce the need for more costly and complex administration routes, such as intravenous delivery, which is seldom used in the hospice setting. The patented device has received 510(k) clearance from the U.S. FDA.

About Brad

Brad Macy is a co-founder, director, and President of Hospi. As a 20-year veteran hospice nurse and a medical device inventor, Brad offers a unique and in-depth perspective on the needs of patients who live with serious or life-threatening illnesses, the caregivers who treat them, and the changing needs of the healthcare industry.

Brad's focus is to guide the company in the development of products inspired by his nursing perspective, such as the Macy Catheter, that enhances patient comfort and wellness, eases caregiver burden, and reduces cost.

Brad received a B.A. in psycho-physiology from California State University, Long Beach in 1987, and a B.S. in Nursing from the University of San Francisco in 1989.

He has also been elected to serve as President of the Bay Area chapter of the Hospice and Palliative Nurses Association for 2014.

For more information, please visit www.hospicorp.com

Discovering Teeth Whitener by Accident

By Tracy Kean

I was inspired when I discovered a cleaning agent in my kitchen

I had burned a pan beyond bad with sugar and I could not get it clean, even with all the cleaners I have -- and I have a lot. I hate to scrub so I started to mix up a concoction from my cabinet. After several tries, I applied it to the pan. WOW did it attack the stain?! Believing that I had found something truly remarkable, I started to test the cleaning product all over my house, discovering new uses. My family and I have been going through tough times, so I thought, "How could I market this to the consumer?"

I read a report by Harvard University that had described the "ideal tooth whitener." I started thinking this could be it, a whitening toothpaste without bleach/peroxide or harsh abrasive levels. It has a gentle pH balance of 7.5 that improved the color up to three shades, offering a full cleaning in 12 days or less, by just brushing your teeth. It would be easy, fast, gentle, and effective. Everyone was going to love it.

For protection, I needed a provisional patent (PP) so I had to get the process down on paper. I researched toothpaste patents and materials commonly used in toothpaste. I had a theory and a formula containing the cleaning agent. You may be thinking at this point that I hold a degree in chemistry or something, but no. I have 18 months or so of college, mostly math courses from 30 years ago. With the internet, you can do anything; it's amazing how much information is available. I also love to bake and have been developing my recipes for years, another skill in the toolbox, including selling millions of dollars of airline tickets.

With the PP in hand, I started selling to As Seen on TV. I got a hit right away through email asking me all kinds of questions about the product and who I was. Then he asked, "Are you a dentist?" I replied "No." That was the last I heard from him. I knew I needed more!

Shortly afterward, I was watching a TV show that highlighted using a university to evaluate your product as an inexpensive way to get a second opinion. I jumped into action, finding a top-ranked school program, and sent all the documentation required. The report came back with positive results and it had many outstanding reviews. One of the highlights was the discovery that the whitener was "superior – a noticeable improvement" to all other products or procedures currently available on the market.

The report was invaluable not only with getting help from family and friends but also when hiring a manufacturer. After too many calls to count, I found Eric Ludwig of Telmark Packaging Corp. I have to say that working with Eric has been, and continues to be, wonderful.

The day I got my first manufactured tube was amazing. Not only did I have a product I could test, but the safety information also confirmed its gentle pH balance. Almost everyone I asked to test the product was excited to use it and volunteered to be part of the study. I would like to thank all the volunteers that gave so generously of their time and allowed me to highlight only their teeth. I got lots of laughs and when I run into a volunteer, they always ask can they get more. Even with documented 'before' and 'after' photos and testimonials from our self-study, I still needed more independent laboratory testing from a top dental testing lab. With outstanding lab results, Pro Polish White tm 12-day Deep Cleaning Treatment was born.

By this time, the patent was published and I was ready to start selling, Eric suggested going on LinkedIn, finding groups, making comments, and starting discussions. It worked. Eighteen months ago, I entered a licensing deal (with the same first contact). My whole family was so excited. It would be on TV and I saw it on the shelves in stores. The check came in the mail, realizing the dream.

When it works, it truly can change your life overnight. Sadly, it is not always the right fit. The whole experience has only made me sure that I am on track to achieving the goal and finding the right fit for Pro Polish White.

To get the funding to get the next manufactured order and to have the samples, I needed more money for some of the business start-up costs. On Feb. 18, Pro Polish White went live on the crowdfunding website Indiegogo.com. You can pre-order Pro Polish White for yourself and your loved ones, at the same time helping us to get the inventory to need to bring it to market.

I always knew that I would share the cleaning product too, but I wanted to stay fully focused on the teeth whitener. With the time standing still with post-production work, I still had patent work to do. I love working and being productive. I keep up with LinkedIn and found a discussion group with a lot of inventors, talking about licensing or selling their invention online to establish a selling record for the product. For example, on Shark Tank, most investors want some kind of track record to "show me the money" before they will sign you.

I went back to the original discovery of the cleaning product. Over the past four years, I continued to use it all over my home. Like with anything else, what it works great on, it's fantastic: cleaning with easy things those other products can't touch like swimming pool tile stains, melting like butter, and simply rinsing away. Identifying and documenting the best attributes and methods for each use was the focus.

Unlike the teeth whitener that requires outsourced manufacturing, I had access to the materials. Once I got my resale number, I needed to duplicate the formula and started the small manufacturing and distributing company TL Kean Co. Over the last several months I have been testing markets and selling methods, such as Amazon, eBay, Facebook, and a website with multiple campaigns, always learning from feedback.

After being successful in marketing the tooth whitener, I have learned to use the feedback to redirect a campaign. I changed the pitch several times before I go get the deal. I've learned how important it is to embrace change, letting go of what's not working and highlighting what is working. Success in a field that is so crowded is hard but doable. Finding a niche market is a good start. Now with inventory ready to sell, the website up and running, and what we think is a great marketing campaign, our new product is here just in time for summer.

The product for sale the focus has changed to marketing to get into pool supply stores for the summer. I know everyone is going to love using Blast LS for its cleaning power but you will be amazed that it cleans without harsh chemicals, odor, or muscle. It's faster and easier than ever before.

I feel so blessed to have made this discovery and to be able to bring both of these amazing cleaning products to life. Over the last few years, I have had the benefit of using both products in my own home, and now you can too.

This is my invention story; the challenges are there and it is so important to keep focused and flexible and to keep going back to the business plan for direction. I love this job, finding new doors to open, removing barriers, and yes, making mistakes, each step gets you closer to the goal.

Holding Cans, Bottles or Anything That Fits!

By Jay Kriner

From an idea started in 2002 in San Marcos, Texas, came a visionary concept of a belt buckle that could retract down and be spring-loaded to hold a beverage hands-free

Since the founder Jay Kriner was unable to afford the patent process at the time, he worked on the concept and design for years, using basic drawing and the finest of "Windows Paint" on his old computer. In 2005, Jay named his idea, "The Beer Buckle"

a.k.a. "BevBuckle!" This same year he quickly bought the web domains and it was all downhill from there. It's been a long and rough road, but a consistent will has driven Jay to follow through on this, one of his many novel ideas.

Presently, Beer Clothing Company, LLC is a clothing and accessory company that holds a

U.S. Patent and many patent-pending designs under its belt. Our most popular design, "BevBuckle!" is an amazing retractable beverage-holding belt buckle. This is not just a caddy novelty item, but a functional fashion accessory that has already found its way into the wardrobes of many people across the U.S., including many popular musicians.

In 2012, our buckle has quickly become the hottest selling accessory across the U.S. By targeting multiple industries including sports, motorcycle, and lifestyle, our buckle, style, and culture have changed the fashion world completely!

The goal is to provide quality products to those who desire to set themselves apart from everyday trends and to distinguish their individuality. Yes, we may set a new trend, adapt to a current trend, translate a past trend, but when you create a mixture, you express your art, and that's our TREND!

About Jay the Inventor

Born in 1981 into a military family, Jay has lived all across the United States. At a young age, he found that he was interested in tinkering, making things and events out of nothing. Creativity came early, and for that and all that he is, he thanks his family and a high school teacher that introduced him to engineering.

Since high school in south Texas, Jay has studied college courses in medical biology, engineering, art, and business. It wasn't confusion, but pure interest in each field that drove Jay to learn as much as he could, hence he is a certified emergency medical technician, unexploded ordnance technician, artist, inventor, patent holder, pitchman, and now an entrepreneur.

"I'm often called crazy for adding new things to my plate of ideas, but without all of them, I wouldn't have learned. Now, you'd think I'm crazy for not doing more," Jay says.

"I never thought this all would be happening, but yet I believed. Having an idea and making it a reality is in no way easy with the hurdles of funding and getting it in front of consumers. It takes real dedication, passion, massive mental support, and borderline obsessiveness."

One key thing he has used to excel is time management and straight out-of-the-box creativeness in the means of PR, design, promoting while creating ROI, and how to separate yourself from the norm or the competition. For inventors, his recommendation would be to jot the idea down and make a real note about it, then revise and repeat. At minimal, contact a friendly, educated, and successful patent attorney to simply discuss the next steps you may need to take. (Email creates a great record.) The rest is home and leg work, so expect years of the unknown and learning.

Having major investors can expedite things, but in reality, for the rest of us, use what you can and reinvest 100 percent over and over again. In no time, you'll be floored by what you've created.

www.BevBuckle.com

As seen on ABC's Shark Tank

Gyro Heat Technologies

By Eric Krohn

I am from Binghamton NY, the birthplace of IBM, LINK, and other revolutionary businesses

I am a Culinary Institute of America; Hyde Park graduate who later went back to school for a degree in nutrition and dietetics. My day job while I continue to progress my technology, is running a grant-funded nutrition program for persons living with HIV/AIDS across eight counties of New York. My job affords me both a set schedule and spiritual wealth, two things that have been vital in my efforts.

I grew up wishing to be involved in new technology development, like my father the famous engineer. However, I did not commit to walking this path as I was never able to easily work with numbers as I might with words or concepts. As life went on and I had accomplished another degree at a later age, I never stopped learning, always reading books, attending lectures, finding teachers in mechanical science, combustion science, law, business, etc.

Four years ago, I was cooking a birthday dinner for my mother when the hollandaise sauce I was preparing was de-emulsified. I passionately attempted to re-emulsify but ended up with scrambled eggs, and a deep disappointment. It was then that I began to see the inherent problem with traditional burners. I realized they all add energy to the same spot on the pan, leaving the job of energy displacement to the cookware, which in turn leads to hot spots and burnt food, burnt cookware, wasted time, and wasted energy as hot spots are over-use of fuel.

Over the next two years, I began the journey of working out how to rotate a flame. At first, I found a partner in a professor at the local university and we spent the following year developing a novel design on paper. During this period, I participated in a pre-seed event, wrote and filed a patent, and committed myself to an Aristotelian life of passionate study and work after my day job, thus eliminating a social life.

When things were starting to look great and manufacturers were being contacted, my partner sent me a message. After talking with a friend and rocket scientist, he learned our design would not work due to an inability to supply ample oxygen to the burner. This short message meant that my design, patent, and any monies spent were for naught. They were wasted and all scrapped. I was devastated and my professor friend also bowed out of the partnership.

I spent the following two months studying like never before. I built other smaller inventions to clear my mind and when I least expected it and it came to me. Now on my own, I was able to see another fault in the traditional heating process that, combined with my rotating burner concept, led to where I am now.

Only 22 percent of the heat from a flame gets absorbed by your cookware or heated object for that matter. So, to restate, 78 percent of the heating process with fire goes to waste in the environment. I wrote a new patent, which now waiting for the United States Patent and Trademark Office (USPTO) to process, and has found ample funding from the Syracuse Clean Technology Garden.

What I invented is a gas burner that utilizes energy-recovery technologies to recycle wasted heat then convert it into electricity. It is now patent-pending, I have a prototype and two more models following this summer. My website and video have been viewed in more than 11 countries and I have received humbling letters from state and federal senators offering support and encouragement.

The process has been nothing short of the greatest roller coaster ride in the field of innovation. I am attempting to reshape how the world heats and cooks. Some don't understand my efforts; some believe it won't be valid for several years, and many more have offered complete support and love for the technology.

No matter how difficult, under-matched, and under-funded someone maybe who sets themselves with the goal of innovating a technology, there is one truth that has led to my success thus far.

Until you quit, you have yet to fail.

Even if the smallest steps are made in progressing your dreams, you will still be ahead of where you were yesterday. Don't be surprised when someday someone helps you take a few faster and larger steps!

The world of innovation is an amazing place, filled with those looking to better the world by fully expressing their dreams. This world is free and accepting to all. Your only cost is what it takes to continue.

The T1 Pro Race Belt

By Brian Mansker

In 1998, I did my first triathlon and from the first swim stroke, I was hooked on the sport

I started to race every time I could get away. As I traveled, I fell in love with the triathlon community, and some of my closest friends came from within it. As I started a family and a career, I was limited on the races I could travel to, but I never lost the passion for the sport of triathlon.

When my oldest child, Coral, became old enough to race in kid's triathlons, she was on board from the beginning. Being in a year-round swim program at Drury University since she was four, she was eager to try this sport since it involved swimming. One of her first races was in Nixa, Missouri (one of the greatest run smaller races around). While there, she had an amazing experience and met an avid, young triathlete named Hannah. Hannah's parents told us about the Ironkids triathlon series, and from the first race, our entire family was hooked.

Eventually, my son Cameron started racing and in 2009 he participated in the Ironkids National Qualifier in Oklahoma City. Even as he came out of the water second and family and friends were cheering him on, it broke my heart as I had to stand by and watch him fumble with his race belt. He's an extremely competitive kid and knows that every second counts in the transition area. He struggled to get it buckled and lost several seconds, leaving on the bike noticeably frustrated.

After that race, I started watching people in the transition area and noticed that almost everyone struggled with the race belts, no matter if they were 8 or 80. I started searching the internet for a better race belt that did not have the cheap plastic snap buckle. To my surprise, every race belt on the market used some form of that plastic buckle. That is when I set out to make the best and fastest magnetic race belt in the world. I started to build prototypes and came up with the perfect race belt after about 20 different prototypes.

At that point, I wanted to fast-track this belt and started calling friends to help me make this dream a reality. I called my friend Scott, an engineer, and he was excited about this project. After calling a patent attorney, we were well on our way to making this happen.

After a lot of sleepless nights and a lot of testing and racing with prototypes, we introduced the world's fastest race belt, the T1 Pro Race Belt. It has 26 pounds of pulling pressure and it allows for any athlete to quickly put it on. My kids have not lost any more precious time in the transition area! My wife, Dawn, and our three kids (Coral, 12, Cameron, 9, and Karis, 6) have a passion for triathlon and we can't wait for you to experience the speed of the T1 Pro Race Belt!

We have come a long way since this story has been shared on InventionStories.com. We have innovations in all of our race belts (we now have the softest webbing of anybody in the industry and the only race belt with a polymer gripper system). We are currently launching a new pocket system belt that is more innovative than anything on the market.

Our belts are now in more than 100 stores in the United States and we have distributors in 11 countries. Last year we were the official race belt of the military triathlon national championships, long-course triathlon national championships, and duathlon national championships.

This year we are the official race belt of the ITU long-course world championships and the USA triathlon off-road triathlon national championships. And we look forward to growing this brand internationally and within the US.

For more information, please visit our website at t1belt.com

The Water Fence - When it Rains, It Stores

By Steven McDowell

Like many of the great ideas of our time, the Water Fence was the brainchild of a young man with a vision

Rainwater harvesting is not new; it has been done for thousands of years. What is new is my concept for storing it with the Water Fence System.

Fresh clean water is California's most precious resource and it seems that we never have enough to go around. As we all know, we are now living in one of the most severe droughts in California's recorded history. With climate change affecting our rain patterns, we must now plan for the possibility of living with far less annual rainfall, so saving every drop could be essential.

Every year, my school has a science fair competition in which every student picks a subject and creates an experiment and/or project, and researches it. Some work in teams; I chose to work alone.

I decided to use California's drought as my subject focusing on how to help solve it, using roof runoff as my source for the water. I wanted to concentrate on each person doing their share and preserving and storing as much water as possible.

Working alongside my father, I visited Friedman brothers, Home Depot, and Lowes Home improvement stores to see what they had available for water storage. The options were all extremely limited. Your only choice was a 50-gallon barrel, which does not store enough to effectively curb water usage.

I went home and researched additional water storage options. I did find large water tanks for storage, but all of the tanks with applicable storage capacity were huge, with many being up to 18 feet tall and more than 12 feet around. These were too big, hard to move around, impossible to fill, and ugly to look at, so all in all they were not very practical.

I knew then that I would have to come up with a completely different solution. I walked around my neighborhood, looking for ideas and what every house had in common so that everyone could participate in storing their water effectively. Then it hit me. Everyone had a fence around their yard and, for the most part, they all were made of the same thing -- wood. I had an idea. What if the fence around my yard could be used to collect runoff rainwater!?

I searched the internet for a product like this and found nothing like it at all. I wanted to know how much water I could store in a fence the size of one around my residence, which is 80 feet by 70 feet by 80 feet. By making my fence pieces the same size as my fence, six feet high by seven feet long and only slightly wider, 12 inches, each fence section held approximately 320 gallons.

By using the standard math formula, 2000 square feet of roof (surface area) multiplied by 1 inch of rain, times the conversion factor, equaled around 1,200 gallons of water runoff. Also, anytime it rains, my fence added water to each storage unit.

I realized that it could hold almost 13,000 gallons of fresh pure rainwater.

I started designing my project to look like a fence and decided on clear plastic so I could show how water seeks its level and would fill each fence section at the same rate. I connected each piece and drilled holes near the bottom to allow water to flow between them.

I completed an original design for the Water Fence and tested it; I knew it worked and entered it into my high school's science fair competition. I won first place!

My engineering teacher stated it was the best original idea he had seen in 14 years of science fairs. My science professor told me to patent the idea right away, which I did. Three of the judges approached me as well and asked me to install it in their homes immediately. I knew I must be on to something.

I entered my project at the Sonoma County Science Fair and won first place!

I then entered it in the San Francisco Bay Area Science Fair and won first place, the U.S Stockholm Junior Water Prize Regional Award, and the American Meteorological Society's "Certificate of Outstanding Achievement! Also, a small group of project creators was invited to a prestigious science fair called The Amgen Bay Area BioGENEius Challenge.

All of these science fairs were judged by accredited scientists, not parents of entrants. After much acclaim, I realized that this product needed to become a distributable reality, fast.

The journey to design, prototype and build the Water Fence has been quite a love of labor. I'd like to thank everyone involved along the way and continue to stress the importance of creating sustainable options for water conservation. In time, I hope the Water Fence will become the industry standard, leading to reduced emissions and freshwater abundance wherever your home is.

How it works

Genuinely efficient. Incredibly effective.

The Water Fence is a truly inspiring housing product designed to allow you to save money and protect our nation's valuable water supply through effective conservation.

As the general population continues to grow, we consume more and more of our freshwater supply, and currently, California's freshwater resources are strained beyond their capabilities. The Water Fence aims to fix this.

Innovative, this new freshwater storage system utilizes roof rain runoff into an interconnected fence system that can store thousands of gallons of water, giving you the possibility of water sustainability, even in severe drought situations. We can't do anything about when it will rain but we do know it will rain again, and it is up to each individual to do their share in preparing and saving every drop. Every time it rains, you add water to your system.

The patented Water Fence System works very simply, as the water runs off the roof and drains into the fence, it continues to fill any number of fence sections you may have.

To calculate your water savings, take the square feet of your roof x each inch of rain x the conversion factor of .632 to get how many gallons of runoff you get for every inch of rain. In example, a 2,000 square foot roof x 1 inch of rain x .632 = 1,264 gallons of freshwater.

This fence takes the place of your existing wood fence and should last almost forever. It is 100 percent recyclable, made of high-density polyethylene. No more trees ever again have to be cut down for the building of fences, allowing them to do what they do best, absorbing CO_2 out of our atmosphere, and combating global warming.

Water naturally seeks its level and fills each section evenly, and each section holds 320 gallons. When connected, the fence can hold thousands of gallons of fresh pure rainwater.

To distribute the water, just connect a hose to your fence via the already installed spigots. The fence has been professionally engineered to easily withstand the weight of water within it and also has been engineered to withstand most seismic events.

Water Fence is also a terrific fire barrier! The fencing will not burn, forming a fire-resistant wall around your home. With the addition of a small water pump (with a battery backup) and a water-delivery system to your roof, you have a fire suppression system that gives your home a recirculating water supply which is a way of giving your home a fighting chance against floating embers that land on your roof, even when water and power have been shut off.

The design on the fence can be individualized into any design/color that you would like. It can be made to look like a rock wall, or a stone wall, or just about any design you prefer.

Homebuilders or developers can simply send a rendering of the desired fence look of their development and it can be reproduced exactly to what they want.

For more information, please visit www.waterfence.com

Glide Bikes™

By Ed Mondello

In 2004, I took my four-year-old daughter, Samantha, to buy a bike

She excitedly chose a popular character bike and we rushed home to give it a try. The first two outings were disastrous. Uneven sidewalks caused the bike to tip over and the bike was so heavy that I had to extract her from underneath it.

Needless to say, her excitement was replaced with scraped knees and elbows, frustration and tears — not an auspicious start to what should have been a happy and enjoyable experience.

I was convinced that the weight of the steel frame was hindering her ability to control the bike and that the training wheels were delaying the learning process by preventing the feel of balancing. I knew there had to be a better way.

Shortly after that, I saw a children's Balance bike at a bike show. Being an avid mountain biker, I instantly understood its concept and the importance of children learning balance as the first step to riding a bike. I began to look for a Balance bike with solid design and durable construction, but finding none, and being the kind of guy who likes to engineer things, I set out to create one myself.

Building a Prototype

Knowing that the key to the design was enabling balance, I based my first glider prototype on the same geometry as a downhill mountain bike1, with a lower center of gravity to give the rider increased stability and a slower balancing speed. It was handmade out of PVC in my backyard in the suburbs of Boston, while there was still snow on the ground.

PV Gliders in Production

Since that prototype, I perfected the design, making minor adjustments to the steering angle and the seat height, and began manufacturing Glide Bikes™ by hand in my workshop in Wilmington, NC, where I moved in 2005. I was proud to be the only Balance bike designed and manufactured in the U.S.

Design Quality Makes Glide Bikes™ Safe & Fun

In 2007, with volume demands increasing, I moved the manufacturing overseas and switched to alloy composition, producing a lighter weight bike for easier maneuvering and increased durability. I also added a hand brake and foot pegs, similar to those on motorcycles, to give riders a fun way to glide and to help them get used to the feeling of where the pedals will be on a pedal bike.

I tweaked the geometry of the design which resulted in a lower balancing speed; I was extremely excited to discover that Glide Bikes will balance at just 1.5 miles per hour, which means that they are the safest balance bikes on the market.

Still designed in the U.S., I am especially proud that Glide Bikes are made of premium materials and are tested for quality assurance regularly by my children (with a little help from Dad!)

Back in 2004, I knew I was on to something big, and, now five years later, I know what that "something big" is. It's the big smiles on the faces of the Glide Bikes Kids who learn to balance confidently and quickly, all while having fun.

For more information, please visit www.glidebikes.com

The Streetzie's High Heel Bunny Slippers Story

By P. Ohls and Copen D. Aiavolasiti

Long, long ago someone had the heart, imagination, and human insight to create the first pair of bunny slippers

To that person, who I feel must have been an inspired woman, I owe a depth of gratitude for creating one of the most enjoyable feminine shoes ever made. Little did she know what a cultural phenomenon the shoe would become in the 20th and 21st centuries. Women and girls all over the world have an affinity for these slippers. They are synonymous with all the endearing qualities of innocence, youth, fun, whimsy, and personal charm. They are an iconic classic, a celebration of life and femininity.

The invention of Streetzie's High Heel Bunny Slippers has been in the making for many years. They are more than a shoe, more than a product, and more than a business. They are the magical by-product of a special synergy between my daughter and me. As an artist, I am hard-pressed to take full credit for the creation of our shoes. They were modeled after the elegant fashion and inspiration of Streetzie Desire. The paradox of where the idea came from is both enlightening and mystifying at the same time. I believe that the muse deserves the ultimate credit, even if she inspires freely.

After a few years of being on her own, my adult daughter discovered a niche and venue for her passion for performance and theatre. She created the alluring stage persona of Streetzie Desire. She has always been independent and self-motivated in her pursuits. Her courage to persevere through adverse circumstances and not lose heart is admirable. Yet from a mother's perspective, watching a daughter "winging it" out there in the world was both worrisome and wonderful.

From our hometown of New Orleans, I felt the maternal pangs of Streetzie's exploration of her talents. I was experiencing empty-nest syndrome, missing my little girl. During that period of our lives, I often strolled the banks of memory lane. "Where did the time go? Did I do my best for her?" I asked myself the same questions mothers will ask for eternity.

One day, I came across an old audio cassette that I had saved. My daughter was fancifully articulate at a young age and had a profound sensibility of language. She was a highly imaginative storyteller who had created an alter ego named Linda Ellie for her adventure tales with her bunny slippers. I played the recording of my daughter telling a spontaneous story in her sweet five-year-old voice, and it sounded cuter than I remembered it. This is the opening line of her story: "Once upon a time there was a girl named Linda Ellie and her two cute little bunny slippers who looked very, very mad!"

She had a dramatic way of tending to her emotions and discerning life lessons on her own through the relationship of Linda Ellie and her slippers. The story brought back vivid memories of what those pink fuzzy little slippers meant to my daughter. They were an intimate source of self-assurance. They were the friends who were always on her side and were always there when she needed them.

They listened with complete understanding. They tickled her imagination and brightened her day with their simple perfect felicity. They were even surrogates for the warm-blooded pets she could not have. She wanted to wear them everywhere. Needless to say, she wore them out.

Finally, after trampling through wet mud in search of frogs and critters in our back yard, they were beyond repair. It was heartbreaking. We found a new pair to replace them. Eventually, she grew fond of those too, but they were never quite as wonderful as the first pair.

In hindsight, I realized that of all the toys and material objects in my daughter's childhood that had contributed to her positive growth and her personal development of character, those dear little personified bunny slippers were the most important.

Through her childhood, I sewed costumes, helped build stage props, and guided her development of a broad range of skills. The fine line between nurturing a child's talents and interfering with them is a delicate matter. Sometimes I crossed that line, and the sense of accomplishment she would have derived from the experience was missing. Now Streetzie grew free of such limitations a mother might impose. Streetzie was soaring to new heights!

Even though my daughter frequently called to share the joys and challenges of Streetzie's stage experiences, I still missed the direct contact I used to have with her world. My nostalgic memories of her performances as a child began to closely coincide with the current events of her career.

Once she needed a spectacular pair of shoes for one of Streetzie's performances. I intended to make a pair of shoes that would add something special to that performance. I would surprise my daughter with a gift that would demonstrate to her how much I believed in her artistry and supported her efforts. I wanted to create something that would convey to her that regardless of the distance between us, I was with her in spirit, and something to remind her of her inner beauty.

Seeking inspiration, I went through some old photographs of her first dance school review at the old New Orleans Municipal Auditorium. I suppose this would be generally considered the defining moment of our invention. I looked at photos of my little girl in her sequined tap shoes and her satin ballet toe shoes. I began to relive the experience.

Humorously speaking aloud, I asked, "Okay, Linda Ellie, tell me what sort of shoe would make Streetzie most happy to dance in now?"

Suddenly I remembered being backstage at that dance review long ago. I was rushing to take off her bunny slippers and put on the tap shoes she was to wear for the performance when she expressed to me, "Mom, I wish I could dance in my bunny slippers." Although I remembered her words, it was as if I were hearing them for the first time! I thought about what I could do to add some glamour and sex appeal to a pair of bunny slippers and make them more suitable for a woman.

That was the epiphany! I felt the metaphorical light bulb flash above my head! The concept of a bunny slipper with high heels was born. My daughter's reaction to the concept was no surprise. It was the same familiar elation I'd seen her express while wearing her first pair of bunny slippers.

The construction of the shoe was not completed in time for the performance. That was a bit of divine intervention in my estimation. Later, my daughter recognized the potential for this shoe concept to become an extremely popular product on the international market. We talked about whether or not we had the wherewithal for such a grand project. We researched every aspect of such a venture. We were committed to putting our invention on the market for a long time. Yet, it was such a reversal of our work orientation that we decided to move on it slowly and carefully.

When Hurricane Katrina devastated New Orleans, it seemed like the right time to follow the winds of change. I sold my property there and we began to work more consistently on getting our shoes to market. My daughter moved from Atlanta to Manhattan to work on her acting career and prospects for our shoe project. Meanwhile, I remained in New Orleans completing the construction of our shoe. It would become the prototype used in the patenting and manufacturing processes.

That year was full of serendipity. The cosmos was sending us affirmation in every direction we turned. Among other good fortunes in Streetzie's career, she landed a small part on a TV show called Fashionably Late with Stacy London. On the first day of filming the series, when my daughter first saw the background set design for the show, she called me and said, "Mom, I know our shoe project is going to be a success. You would marvel at how synchronous this TV show is with our project!"

She couldn't disclose information about the show, but I knew by the tone of her voice it must have been something significant. When the show aired on TV and I saw the wall of shoes for a set design, I was thrilled. My daughter was working with Stacy London, the "Shoe Guru"!

During the first episode, there was a segment about some innovative new design elements in ladies' shoes. The uncanny coincidences seemed surreal to us. We had wondered what Stacy would think of our invention or if she even liked bunny slippers in the first place. To our surprise, my daughter noticed Stacy wearing a pair of bunny slippers behind the scenes. My daughter met many wonderful, talented people while working on the show. It was a valuable, rewarding experience.

When the show was over, Streetzie resumed her status as a freelance entertainer. To a young actress, what could compare to being in New York and on the verge of celebrity? Our shoe project was beginning to appear lackluster by comparison. My daughter was facing a tough dilemma. Should she postpone our mutual project in favor of immediate gratification in her career or should she put her career on the back burner? I was never so grateful for my good fortune to have such a beautiful daughter as I was when she chose the altruistic path. She moved back to New Orleans so we could see our shoe project to fruition.

There are many details to this story which I have not mentioned....so many, so extraordinary, so cosmically custom made, that I would be remiss not to add that the entire endeavor of bringing our shoe to market has an overtone of being on time to an appointment with our destiny.

We are happy to bring you Streetzie's High Heel Bunny Slippers! May they awaken the eternal feminine divine in your spirit. May they remind you of your inner beauty. May they add a magical kick to your stride. May they bring lightness to your being. May they whisper to you all the innocent secrets of happiness. May they serve to strengthen the bonds between women everywhere. It is our wish that you may discover the paradox and join the celebration!

Long live the bunny slipper!

We added a new line, which will feature cats, poodles, black sheep, leopards, and more. Our bunnies have gotten a bit of a make-over as well. The new style slipper will stay true to our original vision while adding a slightly higher heel and modest platform for a bit of extra glamour.

As always, the biggest challenge will be finding the right manufacturer to produce the look. It's challenging enough to source the right materials but creating a shoe that has a toy element makes this a particularly daunting task. In the past, we were unable to find manufacturing that met our needs, leading us to make every pair by hand. In 2016, we tried a different approach to have a fully produced product ready to sell.

We seek co-branding and licensing opportunities if we find that we are not able to meet demand. Although this can be challenging, we know that sometimes you need a little help from brands that have procured top-quality manufacturing and marketing.

If I could give one bit of advice to anyone out there just starting their journey through the wonderful world of invention, I would tell them to follow their heart and be patient! To invent is to pave and create a new road. This will always be a longer journey than taking the road most traveled but the journey itself is magical and enlightening if you are willing to give it time.

More information on Streetzie's High Heel Bunny Slippers and where to purchase them can be found at

www.streetzieshighheelbunnyslippers.com

Solar Powered LED Christmas Lights

By Dawn Ottman

In January 2002, I was visiting my parents

Mom and I were sitting at the dining room table when Dad came in from getting the mail. He put it in front of Mom and when she opened the electric bill, she got upset. It was high because of the big, beautiful display of Christmas lights Mom and Dad had put on the house and in the front yard the past holiday season and it was about to cost them a fortune in electricity.

Mom exclaimed, "Ah, for Christ's sake," then she looked right at me and said, "You're a scientist! Can't you do anything about this?" So, I set to find an answer to the question, "Are solar-powered Christmas lights possible?"

At the time, we didn't have strings of LED lights from a common solar panel on the market. Although this was a great idea, I didn't go in that direction. Instead, I set my sights on creating an individual, independent light: a Christmas light that would stand on its own and not require electric power from an AC outlet.

It had to have its power source and, being an engineer working on satellite electrical power systems that use solar energy, I wondered if a solar panel would work. Besides its power source, my light would need its storage, and that storage needed to be rechargeable so I needed a really small rechargeable battery. LED Christmas lights were already on the market and they would provide a load that had small demands so my light's load would be a LED light.

It seemed fairly elementary to me as the items I had chosen all worked in DC (direct current). The source (the solar panel) is a DC source and the storage (the battery) is a DC storage device providing output to a DC load (the LED light). "How hard could it be," I thought, "And why hadn't anyone thought of it before me?" That's the way it works with inventing.

At the time, I was working for a large data storage corporation so I delved into inventing this light only on weekends. The idea of making inventing a full-time job came to me due to unforeseen life events.

You see, in 2003, I fell down some stairs and became disabled. No longer able to work a normal 9-to-5 job and broke from paying medical expenses, I moved to South Dakota where I could afford to live off my military pension. When I was home shopping, I found a gem and I ended up buying myself a garage to invent out of. Luckily for me, it came with a house too!

But let me tell you about the garage from heaven. It was amazing: oversized two-car garage, insulated and heated, with a workbench and cupboards for storing parts and equipment in. It was PERFECT!

After I researched and developed my idea, I had no problem developing the prototype myself then testing it. My background in test engineering made this a fairly easy task for me. Yet, the business world wanted to see independent verification testing done and so I hired an engineering firm to do this. It cost me six months of my military pension and I got nothing from it. The firm screwed up by using an IC (integrated circuit) that was physically too large for my design and this IC had a bridge voltage greater than the thin-film solar panel put out. This IC was designed for medium voltage applications and not for micro voltage applications such as my invention. Talk about throwing away money.

If that wasn't enough to get me down, know that I have not had much success in marketing my patent. I believe it is because I just don't know how to do this. A few years ago, I hired a marketing manager who brought me a good patent sale offer to a Chinese firm. I wanted to have this be an American-made product. And, although the money was good, I would have felt as if I had sold out American jobs, so I said no.

Later when I had a feasibility study done, I learned that all Christmas and holiday-themed manufacturers are in China. I became concerned about this news so I arranged for my patent to be submitted to China's Intellectual Property Office and my patent has now been issued in China.

Still, it was obvious that I do not have business savvy. But what I do have is a heart and a strong desire to create American jobs. Some days I regret my product not already being on store shelves but I believe that all good things come to those who act on their beliefs. So, I've stood fast and I believe that as technology advances, my light will last longer and we'll all be better for it.

Deciding on a manufacturer has been an extremely challenging road. This is not my forte, as you will see. Once I learned that there are 2,000 Christmas light manufacturers in China and none in the USA, I had a necessary change of heart.

Disappointed in my marketing manager, I fired him even though he was doing was his job by bringing me offers for my intellectual property, which rejected for not being made in America. I was pigheaded.

So, now I had to go on my own. First, I met with a Chinese manufacturer with an office based out of Denver. Their products (14 million strands of lights sold in 2007) were not manufactured in the USA so I begged for distribution jobs here yet the company was adamant that all distribution jobs would be done out of China. We were at an impasse and I walked away from their generous offer.

I was in a quandary about what to do. How could little old me help create jobs in the USA? Could they be the sort of manufacturing jobs that did integration? The next road I considered taking was to use parts from China and do the integration and distribution here in the USA, but I needed investors. I met with a Dakota-based company. Although they thought my idea had merit, they became uncommunicative and I later learned it was because of profit margins.

You see, there was profit to be made if we did the integration process here, but the profit margins were much larger if everything was done in China. What I took away from this was the understanding of profit margins and a bit more about the manufacturing process.

It was obvious to me that manufacturing would have to be done in China. My next effort was to do the manufacturing in China myself. So, I hired a middleman and he recommended a manufacturing factory in the Guangdong Province in China. I was set to fly to China to meet with the manufacturing team he was putting together and to approve the sample when my attorney got back to me. We had a connection in China because I had patented there, and I had my attorney do an investigation on the selected factory and the report was disheartening. This factory had no experience in making electronics and was instead only a plastic mold factory. So, I walked away.

I'd like to say that I learned something valuable from that experience but I didn't. For the next few months, I worked on my next patent while thinking about what to do with this one. Maybe I should just sell the IP? So, I hired a firm that sells intellectual property but I was unhappy with the lack of results they brought to me.

So, not one to give up I next looked into manufacturing in Mexico. I had heard how in the mid-1990s almost all manufacturing in Mexico was moved to China but that now it was moving back and the Mexican government was looking for opportunities. Maybe that opportunity would be the manufacturing of my lights. It looked promising so I opened up discussions with the Mexican government. Then I learned that the Guadalajara area where the Mexican government was considering was also a stronghold of the Mexican cartel. Okay, so I'm not doing that! Since then, I've just spent a lot of time scratching my head.

As you follow your path to being an inventor, people will say, "That won't work." But if you believe it does, don't listen. Some people see things and say, "Why?" But I dream of things that never were and say, "Why not!" In my previous work life as an engineer, I've come across things that don't work and it was my job to make them work. Technological advances happen every day so dream big and go for it!

I remember when I was being interviewed to work on the Iridium Satellite Program with Motorola, the manager told me something about the satellite's capability that was not possible. I remember losing interest rather quickly.

He noticed! "What?" he asked me and I knew my body language had given me away. I answered him, saying, "You can't do that." "Why not?" he asked and I answered, "Because the technology isn't there!"

His response to me had me signing on the dotted line to work for Motorola. What he said was, "You're right, but it'll be there when we get there!" I loved the fact that there were still some challenges to face and overcome.

Inventing is so worth the effort and it is such interesting work, but my advice would be to work with someone who has some business savvy. Still, I have found that inventing something is its reward. Who knows what tomorrow will bring?

Hybrid Wind Turbine

By Dawn Ottman

I had learned a great deal about amorphous silicon photovoltaics (thin-film solar) as I worked through my Solar Powered Christmas LED Light invention

I did not spend all my time inventing.

While working on these ideas, I enjoyed a few opportunities to teach about renewable energy and energy conservation. When I was selected to be a National Wind Senator, I headed to New York State to get a deeper understanding of wind energy and how to teach kids about it. While there, I learned how the wind turbine farm uses up a lot less land than a solar farm does while producing a lot more energy. And that's when I got the idea about combining the two renewable energy technologies.

Hybrid wind energy turbines were already being co-located on solar energy farms so the power was already being combined (that is there was a hybrid output). Because crystalline silicon solar panels are very heavy while thin-film ones are not, the thin film would be used by my invention. Also, the crystalline silicon solar panels (the ones you see on the roofs of buildings and houses) are rigid while the thin film (amorphous silicon) is not. They are so flexible; they are often delivered like a rolled-up carpet. So, I thought, why not unroll the carpet and put it on the wind turbine towers.

First, I had to look at the output power of the amorphous silicon and the surface area on the tower structure so I could calculate what the output power would be. It wasn't much when compared to the wind turbine's output but it had one distinct advantage when the wind didn't blow and during the long daytime hours, it would have an output. Any output is better than no output but it also added to the output of the wind turbine when it was producing power. Their combined output from multiple wind towers would be beneficial. BONUS!

Initially, I approached General Electric when I started to market it. I have a friend there who is a fellow engineer. I believed GE would be interested in my idea as they were in the process of building an amorphous silicon solar manufacturing plant in Colorado. This would be an awesome marriage of their technologies (solar and wind). They were already a recognized leader in the wind power industry and their wind turbine manufacturing capability is well known.

But investors want to know about something known in the financial world as return on investment (ROI). This is important stuff. When an investor is putting money into something, they want -- no, they need -- to see a return. This means not only on the money invested but the money that investment makes.

GE responded to me saying they weren't interested at this time.

I turned to other wind turbine manufacturers but they each had their wind turbine tower suppliers (like GE did). Imagine my excitement when I learned that a wind turbine tower manufacturer had selected South Dakota (my home state) for a new manufacturing facility. I immediately approached this company, but Marmen was not interested in this technology or any new advances to the tower. I was told they were happy with the business they were doing and they weren't interested in new ideas, including mine. I was bummed!

The next path I took was looking at making my invention more attractive by having a prototype of it but that would be a large and expensive process. I knew I would need financial help.

So, I applied for a Small Business Innovation Research National Science Foundation (NSF) Grant. I arranged to work with Arizona State University (ASU) and Mitchell Technical Institute (MTI) to define the optimum configuration and define the ROI. The plan was to work with ASU's renewable energy group who would do the data collection and analysis and MTI would provide the wind turbine tower as well as the wind turbine technicians to install and monitor the solar PV and collect data on the power production. If all went well with this application, NSF would provide the funding.

We were not funded by the National Science Foundation and the whole thing fell apart. There are many obstacles along the way and the process of bringing your invention to the light of day requires tenacity.

Restart Power Using Hybrid Wind Turbine

Undaunted, I turned to my thinking outside the box mentality and I was able to define a new use for the solar PV on the wind turbine tower and use it as wind turbine restart power.

At the National Renewable Energy Lab in Colorado, I had learned that wind farm operators are installing diesel generators in their wind turbines to restart the turbines after a storm has passed. Diesel generators are a maintenance nightmare, require the storage of diesel on-site, and they are certainly not a renewable energy solution to the challenge of restarting wind turbines.

After confirming the output of the solar on the tower does provide the required power to restart a wind turbine, I submitted another patent to the United States Patent and Trade Office (USPTO). That patent is now pending. (More details on the next page.)

I just keep plowing along, working on new ideas with the knowledge that one day, this technology will be needed. Until then, I keep a close eye on advances in the technologies I've used in my inventions. Be assured that inventing is not for the faint of heart.

The System and Method for Restarting a Wind Turbine Using Clean Energy

By Dawn Ottman

CanDew Scientific is a company that is dedicated to "green" engineering, located in South Dakota

There is a new wind turbine restart power invention that uses renewable energy. In many cases, hybrid energy epitomizes the advantages of additive power – combining different energy forms – in circumstances and environments where a single energy form is unable to provide power reliably or cost-effectively.

According to the National Renewable Energy Laboratory, diesel generators are being used to restart wind turbines during power outages. Using a non-renewable energy source (diesel generators) to restart a renewable energy source (wind turbines) just seems wrong.

CanDew Scientific is steadfast in its commitment to research and creating products based on renewable energy. Our company has invented a fix and is the proud owner of U.S. Patent Serial No. 14/695,795 which is a patent for a System and Method for Restarting a Wind Turbine Using Clean Energy.

Now, using this new invention, it no longer makes economic sense to use diesel generators to supply a wind turbine's restart power. Just some of the benefits and significant technological advantages of this intellectual property include the increase of the dependability of wind energy as an energy source, the decrease in the Life Cycle Material Management (LCMM) of a wind farm, and the increase in the availability of wind energy. These advantages impact the bottom line as they increase the profitability of a wind farm which is an important business point.

This patent's systems and methods decrease potential dangers and hazards inherent in the handling of diesel generators. Within the LCMM of using diesel generators are the needs for delivery of the diesel, storage of the diesel onsite, and the manpower to ensure the safe and proper turn-on of the diesel generators when they are needed. In comparison, the solar system of this invention can be controlled and managed electronically and remotely.

Further advantages result from the physical placement of the flexible solar panels on the wind turbine structure. No additional land will be needed for this solar system. Solar energy is generated by a network of flexible solar panels attached to the wind turbine tower, which is an important advantage for off-shore wind farms. Also, the solar system uses flexible solar panels such as amorphous silicon (thin-film solar) or power plastic solar panels; both of which have long life spans.

Perhaps most exciting is that when the solar energy is not being used to restart the wind turbine, it augments the output power of the wind turbine. When the blades are stationary, the solar panels continue to provide an output. This is most clearly underlined by the advantages of combining solar and wind – where solar performs best during the day and wind provides greater energy at night.

The race for renewable energy has passed a turning point. The world is now adding more capacity for renewable power each year than coal, natural gas, and oil combined. And there's no going back. The shift occurred in 2013 when the world added 143 gigawatts in new plants that burn fossil fuels, according to an analysis presented Tuesday, April 21, 2015, at the Bloomberg New Energy Finance annual summit in New York.

The shift will continue to accelerate, and by 2030 more than four times as much renewable capacity will be added. The reason solar will soon dominate is that it is a technology, not a fuel. As time passes, the efficiency of solar power increases, and prices fall, unlike oil which is not renewable: once it is used, it is used up.

The Tibbe-Line Can Save You Time and Much More

By Rose Pacheco

Tibbe-Line is not a complicated invention

It's not high-tech and it's not the next candidate for a fashion fad. Instead, it's simple and its inventor, Rose Pacheco, says it saves time and electricity.

A cosmetologist by day, Pacheco has invented a flexible plastic sleeve that slides over a clothesline or other rope and allows a person to hang clothes hangers on it.

The sleeves, each measuring 13 inches long, have holes drilled in them for the hanger hooks so that all the clothes don't slide together at the clothesline's lowest point. They work for drying clothes and for storing clothes anywhere someone can rig up a line. It's a simple little device, but Pacheco thinks it has a huge future by allowing people to air-dry their clothes easily while using less electricity and time.

"People who have bought my Tibbe-Line call or write me and they're so excited about doing laundry," the energetic Pacheco said. "They're excited because they're saving time."

The Tibbe-Line retails for $14.95 for a pack of three, enough to hold 21 hangers across 39 inches of space.

Pacheco says there's nothing on the market like it. "It hasn't taken off yet, but I believe it will," she said of her product, named for her maiden's name of Tibbe. "It's like a dam that has a little hole in it."

Time is important to Pacheco, a cosmetologist who works with home-bound people and who also makes balloon arrangements for special occasions and events. She's a super- energetic 60 years old and confesses that she has a hard time not being constantly in motion.

"I've worked just about my whole life," the Pueblo native said, "at the IRS, the Army Depot, the Bureau of Land Management, the Forest Service, I've done a lot of different things. The only time I find that I can stay still is when I'm reading the Bible. Otherwise, I'm always doing something."

Her hard work with the Tibbe-Line is not surprising. She's taken the device to trade shows, demonstrated it to college students at Colorado State University-Pueblo, and is contacting 2,000 additional colleges and universities to see if she can convince students there to buy it, too.

"I had never been in a college dorm," she said about when she first visited the university to drum up business for the Tibbe-Line. "I walked in and I couldn't believe it. It was 12 feet by 12 feet with two little beds, two little dressers, and two inky-dinky closets." Because she markets the Tibbe-Line as a laundry aid and a storage device, Pacheco saw an opportunity. "My Tibbe-Line would be perfect," she said.

The Tibbe-Line was born shortly after Pacheco was doing laundry one day in 1996. She likes to air-dry her clothes, but some need to be placed on a hanger first to dry without being distorted. Pacheco hung her clothes on a clothesline the regular way with clothespins, then hung a heavy denim shirt on a hanger and hung that in the eye-bolt holding up the clothesline. A strong wind that day blew most of Pacheco's clothing to the ground, but the denim shirt "was just whipping around in the wind and didn't fall," she said.

Later, Pacheco caught herself looking at a door hinge and that's when she says the Holy Spirit touched her and the whole idea all fell into place: a plastic device that could be closed around a clothesline and hold hangers at regular intervals.

Pacheco loves her invention because she likes to dry her clothes in the dryer for a short time to remove much of the water, then hang the clothes damp on hangers and let them air-dry.

She's cut her laundry time dramatically, she says, because she doesn't have to wait for the entire dryer cycle to finish. It also saves wear and tear on the clothes and saves electricity, which Pacheco sees as a major selling point.

When she made the first Tibbe-Line, people didn't care as much about global warming and saving energy, she said. But now, "when you turn the TV on, at least once a week that subject comes up. There is nothing, nothing, nothing like this!"

Bringing an invention from idea to reality, then actually selling it, is a famously hard and long process. The inventing landscape is littered with the corpses of ideas that someone just couldn't get to catch on to.

Pacheco said it's taken her at least six years and $25,000 to bring the Tibbe-Line to life. After she had her idea, Pacheco says she got a lot of timely help from other people getting it made. She already was going to the Pueblo Community College Campus' Small Business Development Center to discuss applying for a small-business loan for her cosmetology work.

When Pacheco asked for help on her Tibbe-Line, someone at the development center directed her to PCC engineer and teacher Chris Washington, who was nice enough to draw up plans for the Tibbe-Line from Pacheco's description.

Pacheco then found a plastics manufacturer in Denver that made a batch of the Tibbe- Lines, and after a friend made her a jig for them, Pacheco used a drill press to drill holes in each one herself before packaging them for sale.

"I got to where I could do 100 Tibbe-Lines an hour," Pacheco said.

Pacheco also hired an attorney and, after being rejected twice, obtained a patent for her invention, spending thousands of dollars to do so.

Selling the Tibbe-Lines has taken considerable effort. Pacheco has set up a website and sells some through that venue. She's also traveled a bit to market the device and constantly is honing her pitch and identifying uses for the invention.

While she was at a trade show, one comment she heard, again and again, was that the adults at the show wished they'd had something like the Tibbe-Line when they were in college and short on time, space, and quarters for the dryers. That started Pacheco on her present marketing push with the colleges. And she said she's always finding more uses for the invention. An artist friend likes them for holding painting materials. A teacher uses Tibbe-Lines to hang kids' projects.

"If there's someone who can't find one good reason for using the Tibbe-Line, they must be from Mars!" she said.

Sales are still very modest, but Pacheco keeps at it.

"The only reason is that the Holy Spirit gave me the idea, otherwise I would have probably given up on it." She says each time she's faced an obstacle, something eventually has happened to help her get past it, "and away I go. It is a long, hard road," she said. "You just have to have a lot of tenacity. I remind myself of a pit bull."

More information about the Tibbe-Line and where to purchase it can be found at www.tibbeline.com

Tennis Ball Dryer...an Eco Tennis Accessory that Saves Players Money

By Jason Saunders

After many years of playing tennis, I became aware of a regular annoyance suffered by most tennis players around the world and decided to find a simple solution that everyone could use

When playing outside, tennis courts often retain moisture from recent rainfall, dew, or frost. This plays havoc with our tennis balls. The tennis ball fibers absorb any moisture on the court surface and, if left wet for too long, lose pressure and bounce ability.

Tennis players have all been there. We place our furry wet tennis balls back in their tins until our next match, only to discover they are still wet and have lost their bounce when we re-open the tin days later. The tennis balls are no longer of any use and end up being discarded for new ones. It is an unnecessary waste of our money and time.

Recognizing other players also found this annoying, I researched the topic and found there were no solutions for this problem in the marketplace, other than to just buy new tennis balls every time. There had to be a simple solution that could prevent the waste of good tennis balls, just because they get wet.

Most club and recreational tennis players will use a set of tennis balls between two to six times, so a device that can maintain the longevity of the ball would have great value.

With more than 600 million tennis balls manufactured in the world each year, a solution to save tennis balls must be a good idea not only for saving players money, but also good for the planet.

So, I set about developing an easy-to-use, affordable device that we could all simply put our wet tennis balls into after playing outside and leave to dry until our next match. With tennis balls now costing up to £10/$15 in some shops, this would be useful for every tennis player who plays outdoors.

With my skills as a professional designer and concept visualizer, I set about designing a solution. After two years of development, I designed a special three-layered drying system made from various textile properties and combined them with a clever cord-string-closing mechanism to wrap the drying system around the tennis balls.

Essentially, a three-layered bag that holds four tennis balls and has a drawstring handle that closes the materials neatly around the balls for maximum surface contact and drying efficiency.

I wanted to add more functionality to make it as useful as possible for the tennis player. So, a shoulder strap handle was added to allow for easy carry functionality compared to the awkward ball tins. Discarding the sharp ball tins and using the four-ball bag instead for kids was another worthy consideration for parents.

I then integrated a 914mm net measure marker system to the shoulder strap to allow easy checking of the tennis net height during a match. A fourth function was added to keep drinks bottles cool whilst playing. Simply pop your already cooled drinks bottle into the bag and the cooling properties of the inner bag layer will help maintain the drink to be cool for longer.

The Tennis Ball Dryer was finally conceived: a four-in-one function tennis accessory for every tennis player.

I researched the tennis market and once I was happy with my design and initial working prototypes, I registered my design and concept with the patent office for commercial protection. The drawings were then submitted to a great model-making company (Bang Creations UK) which made a working prototype of my design that could be taken to a manufacturer. With some additional help from MAS (Manufacturing Advisory Service) in the UK to finalize the engineering drawings for manufacturing purposes, it was time to begin production.

After a frustrating six months wasted with factories failing to make a good working product, I finally found a manufacturer that understood how to deliver what was necessary.

The 'Tennis Ball Dryer' was launched in 2010 with great critical acclaim from the tennis press. ACE Tennis magazine awarded Tennis Ball Dryer 'the best tennis gadget of the year' and Tennis Head magazine placed it in their 'Fab Five Tennis Gear list.' I was also interviewed on the BBC evening news to discuss my eco money-saving device.

"Why wouldn't every player want one?" is a quote from customer D. Sandercock who has confirmed it has saved him money several times over on new tennis balls already in one year.

I have now been granted the patent for Tennis Ball Dryer since application and have had thousands of successful sales through my business website www.tennisballdryer.com, but also, across Amazon, where Tennis Ball Dryer has been in the top-three best-selling of all tennis products during December, for two years running.

Moving forward, I would like to partner with a well-known sports brand such as Adidas or Nike that can help sell this on a far bigger scale through a larger distribution and promotional network. My company Aspect Sports has proven there is a market for the Tennis Ball Dryer and I am excited for the future of this product.

Contact Jason Saunders at Aspect Sports via www.tennisballdryer.com

DippyCups

By Lisa Ann Savage

For all of you who have been mulling over a great idea that might make our busy lives easier or put smiles on our children's faces, I share my story with you and encourage you to "JUST GO FOR IT!"

Why I Decided to Make and Sell DippyCups

Like most children, my two kids like to dip their food in sauces, such as ranch, ketchup, and syrup. They eat more veggies when they dip. My son, now 11, was a big dipper and would pour ketchup and ranch on his plate; most of it was wasted and made a big mess for me to clean up. My daughter, now 8, was the opposite; she was the princess who didn't want any sauce touching her food unless she dipped it herself. I needed a way to corral the condiments, so to speak. I tried cutting paper Dixie cups in half but this got expensive and they were too small and got soggy.

Disposable plastic cups were too deep and didn't fare well in repeated dishwasher cycles. Glass or ceramic ramekins are too big and take up too much room on a child-size plate, not to mention they're breakable.

One day, while hunting for yet another little cup, the idea for DippyCups popped into my head. I could build a better DippyCup, one that was just the right size for a kid's plate, the right portion size, unbreakable, made of a material like silicone, that would last, especially if thrown in the dishwasher daily, and in fun bright colors. You could say that was my "Aha moment." I had some prototype DippyCups made and gave them to friends and family members and they all loved them! I was really on to something.

Realistic Expectations

I think my expectations were realistic because I had my priorities straight. I am a single mom and my children always come first. My day job is important to me so I make sure I cover all those bases. Also, my children's father is terribly ill so I take him to chemo, arrange doctor's appointments, deal with his insurance, etc. I'm just like a lot of single moms, somehow, we find a way to fit it in if it needs to be done. I also believe we can only do what we can do and sometimes we have to make tough choices.

DippyCups sat on the back burner for almost two years before I found the time and energy and belief in myself to go for it. As for the process, creating DippyCups was easy because I had a clear idea of what was needed to make the perfect little cup and I was excited about the idea so it drove me in the beginning. My prototype was made at midnight out of Play-Doh. The manufacturing part was relatively easy for me because

I had contacts in the silicone molding industry and sought out their advice.

Promotion of the product is the most challenging part and the one that stalled me for the longest time. How do I get my product out there? Will they like it?

I decided just to take a flying leap and exhibit at the All Baby and Child Show in Las Vegas. Many buyers attend and I thought it would be the perfect place to get feedback on my product. Well, the feedback was wonderful; I had more than 100 people and companies interested in DippyCups! It was such a great validation of my idea. I truly felt blessed. But now the hard work begins, being able to ramp up manufacturing and get packaging in place to fill orders.

Balancing Work and Motherhood

It is challenging to balance work and motherhood for all of us. Many days I wish I could win the lottery and just putter around the house, doing projects, maybe exercising, or catching up on the scrapbooking that I haven't done since my son was six months old. I know my limitations and am not too hard on myself if I can't get something done.

I tend to focus on people instead of things; "someone" that needs attention is more important than "something" that needs attention. At home, playing with my kids at the park comes before folding laundry. At work, getting answers or products for customers comes before internal expense reports and call reports in my day job. Sometimes this causes problems, like a laundry of mountain or an accountant in my case. But most of the time, if I've made the people I care about happy, then that is a good day's work.

Mom Entrepreneur

My kids think it's pretty neat that I am an entrepreneur and I like the message it's sending. If you have a dream, you should follow it through no matter where it leads, you'll learn something. They love using their DippyCups every day and they feel it's kind of their project too because I have enlisted their help along the way. They have helped me choose the DippyCups colors, do product testing, packaging, approved my logo; give ideas for the website, etc. We've had a lot of fun.

My Parenting Motto

Children are only little for such a short while. The only thing they need is your unconditional love so, walk and talk and laugh and play and kiss and hug a lot! (Which is the theme of the children's book I am writing!)

My Advice

I bought a wonderful little plaque in a small neighborhood shop that sums it up for me:

"Sometimes, you just have to take the leap, and build your wings on the way down."

For more information, please visit www.dippycups.com

Sugru Mouldable Glue – the Future Needs Fixing

by Team Sugru

While studying for my Master's degree in Product Design (read 'playing and experimenting with materials') at the Royal College of Art in London, I (Jane ni Dhulchaointigh) had a bit of an idea

February 2003

"I don't want to buy new stuff all the time. I want to hack the stuff I already have so it works better for me." (I didn't say it out loud. I just thought it.)

If I'm honest, the first version of Sugru was pretty horrible — made from smelly silicone caulk and waste wood dust from the wood workshop. But it helped me hack my kitchen sink plug to make it bigger and make a knife more comfortable.

April 2003

The smelly silicone I'd made back in February wouldn't leave me alone. I knew it could be amazing. I pictured it as a kind of space-age rubber — super easy to shape, sticky, and durable. I knew it needed to feel gorgeous and that, if I cracked it, it'd have a million uses. But it was only an idea. I mean, I gave up chemistry in school!

2004

As part of my Final Year Project, I returned to the idea and got excited. This was bigger than just me. I got out my sketchbook and started imagining a world where this material existed.

I knew that, by tapping into people's innate creativity, all kinds of products could be transformed and improved. I knew that we could adapt and improve almost anything mass-produced.

Summer 2004

I refined my prototype material with pigments and finer powders and presented it at my final exhibition. When the most common questions were "How much is it?" and "Where can I get it?' I got even more excited and decided I had to make my concept real.

October 2004 – May 2005

I started gathering a team of specialists to help me turn this material into a real thing. The first was my partner James Carrigan and my business partner Roger Ashby, then two incredible scientists, Ian and Steve, who had just retired from top jobs in the silicone industry. Then David, an awesome and wise patent lawyer.

June 2005

Nesta, the UK's innovation think tank, awarded the Company a £35,000 Creative Pioneer grant to get off the ground. We drank champagne on a street bench to celebrate.

August 2005

After paying a contract lab £5,000 to do three experiments, I realized the only way to develop this material was to do it myself. With Steve's help, I set up a small laboratory and learned the basics so I could start what would be two long hard years of formulation work.

July 2006

We had our first successful results in our chemical formulations and applied for some patents. This was enough to bring in some investment funding to take the product development to the next level. Thanks to the great guys at Lacomp who believed in us so early on. That night we drank champagne in a little Vietnamese restaurant.

September 2006

Everyone knows a small company can't build a household brand. You need to build a partnership with a big multi-national corporation, right?

Jane and Roger started making friends with the nice people at some of the world's leading glue companies.

December 2006

We started exploring potential industrial uses for our materials with some really interesting brands. For example, we worked on a cold-curing grippy material for garden tools. We worked with a top pencil manufacturer on some concepts for a new super-grippy premium range.

September 2007

We started to get consistently strong and stable materials but making sure the material stuck to lots of other materials was still a big challenge.

January 2008

Our user trial group (mainly our friends) grew to more than 100 people. Their feedback was feeding into our work. Everyone was saying "make it stick to more stuff."

April 2008

The pace of developments with the big companies was extremely slow. My designer friends at Atto Partners had been nagging me for a while, and it began to sink in. I started to feel that maybe we could build our brand. Another friend told me "Start small and make it good." The dream started coming back.

May 2008

Five years later, and I'd never found a good name. One day around now, riding downhill on my bike I thought of the word Sugru, inspired by the Irish word for 'play.' I fell in love with it.

June 2008

Our funding was running low, and we were still a way off with our development. We started pitching for investment again, but it was different this time. The recession meant we pitched to almost 100 investors.

December 2008

With the recession getting deeper, we were scraping by on our overdraft. With no great signs from investors, we hit a low point. Tears were shed.

January 2009

I made a New Year's resolution. Stop listening to other people's advice. Go with my gut.

June 2009

At last, a private investor put up just enough funding for us to launch Sugru ourselves. We set ourselves a deadline of six months to make it happen. It was now or never. We bought a small mixer and working with one of our engineer friends to design a packaging machine, we built it for £5,000 and it ran on an Arduino. We designed a brand to get ourselves excited. We made videos, designed packaging, and built a website.

November 2009

Having converted our lab into a little factory, we spent days and nights making and packing Sugru. All of our friends and family helped. It took an entire month of blood, sweat, tears, and favors to make our first 1,000 packs.

December 1, 2009 (The Day Our World Changed)

We'd sent Harry Wallop at the Daily Telegraph Technology blog a pack to try out. He gave it a 10/10 review. Wired and Boing saw it and linked it to our new website. Things started to go crazy. New links came thick and fast. Our first 1,000 packs sold out in six hours.

December 2, 2009

We put another 2,000 packs up for pre-order. We said that it'd take us months to ship the orders. They sold out in 10 hours. Everything was different now. How could we make more?!

December 3, 2009 – April 2010

All of a sudden, we had our pick of some pretty awesome investors. This influx of money would help us build the factory we needed, and to start building our team. We did just that.

March-May 2010

While we were getting our factory and supply chain up and running, we started getting out and meeting our customers. The Newcastle and Bay Area Maker Faires were our highlights; we loved meeting all the awesome people we'd talked to online.

June 2010

After a six-month ramp-up, we relaunched sales properly with an updated website and a warehouse full of Sugru. In the first week, we shipped to more than 40 countries. A lot of good people had been incredibly patient, and it felt great to share our idea with the world.

July 2010

We started receiving hundreds of stories from new Sugru users all over the world. It was so exciting. This is why I invented Sugru in the first place. We got an email from Rob, who had trekked to the North Pole with Sugru grips on his ski poles. We realized we had customers in six of the seven continents of the world. We asked the community if they had friends in Antarctica who would like some. They did.

September 2010

Our first retailer, the London Design Museum, started stocking Sugru.

November 2010

TIME Magazine listed Sugru alongside the iPad as one of the top 50 inventions of 2010. The iPad was number 34; Sugru was number 22.

December 2010

Team Sugru had grown from two people to six. We had our Christmas party in our new factory. The Sugru community was growing — it was now in over 60 countries! My favorite part of every month was digging through the community's contributions before writing the monthly email update.

June 2011

More than half of our community is in North America, so we set up a company there to speed up shipping, and to supply US-based retailers. Our community hit the 50,000 people mark. We drink pints in our local pub to celebrate.

August 2011

A little film inspired by a hack by a Sugru user gets 50,000 views in a week. It's an amazing idea, and people are further inspired.

September 2011

Sugru has featured in the V&A's amazing exhibition the Power of Making. Team Sugru grows to more than 10 people. All of the community's feedback and photos are showing us what Sugru is good for, and who finds it useful. All of the feedback makes us confident that it's not just for fun — it's a great technical solution.

While continuing to keep community creativity at the heart of what we do, we get focused on bringing Sugru to the next level, where more people can find it when they need it. When their cables break, or the fridge door cracks, or their hiking boots leak.

October 2011

Hack of the month from Rob in Sussex shows us how to make glow-in-the-dark tent pegs with Sugru.

November 2011

We evolve the Sugru website to start sorting hacks, tips, information, and inspiration by interest groups. Lots more work continues behind the scenes. Our network expands to lots of lovely resellers in the UK and the US, and we launch with our first large retail group, allowing customers in 50 UK towns and cities to buy Sugru locally for the Christmas season.

December 2011

The team reaches 15 people and we started to feel like sardines in our space. For months we'd been trying to wrangle the empty unit next door. We finally get the keys!

January 2012

We get lots of snowy images of fixes from the slopes – fixes and mods to snowboards, ski poles, gloves, boots, and helmets. It's awesome to see Sugru being trusted and performing well in extreme situations!

February 2012

We're thrilled that Sugru is one of the 50 winners of 'Britain's new Radicals' – a list compiled by The Observer and NESTA showcasing "the inspiring people and businesses that are changing the UK for the better" Even the UK Prime Minister commented.

March 2012

Hack of the month goes to @Robiot6 on our community forum for her clever thinking: "My fridge is not very practical for our family usage; I was missing a silly 0.5cm to be able to stack our yogurts – Sugru fixed it for me!" A simple and elegant solution that would be difficult to do without Sugru – awesome!

April 2012

In the time since we launched, we'd had hundreds of emails asking for different colors, and the ability to mix a wider range of colors. It wasn't as easy as we hoped but after some great work in the labs, we finally cracked it. Sugru now comes in primary colors!

May 2012

Back in March, a super cool Sugru user called Eimear sent us an image of a Sugru repair she'd just done for one of her students, Foridha, whose wheelchair joy-stick controller kept breaking. It didn't hold up, unfortunately, so around now she got back in touch to ask for help. James was taking the community emails that day, and he noticed the postcode

– Foridha and Eimear were only down the road! He and Ben jumped on their bikes to give them a hand.

June 2012

Our user community expands to more than 100,000 customers and our confidence in Sugru is growing. Our vision from the start has been to help get the world repairing and making again. This means appealing to not only fixers and DIYers, but people who don't yet fix. We decide to bring our mission to the fore, and we evolve our brand and our packaging accordingly. We love our new motto – The future needs fixing.

July 2012

The fix of the month goes to Joanne who reminds us that sometimes a fix can make a big difference, not just a small one. Her heart was set on competing in an epic canoe race up the Yukon River – 700km long. But with no fingers on her left hand, it was looking impossible. A small modification to the paddle allows her not only to compete but to finish the race – after three days and three nights straight paddling. She says she wouldn't have been able to do it without the mod. We're blown away!

August 2012

Being based in London, we've been getting excited about the Olympics for quite a while. We've also been working on a secret project with Leon Paul London, a leading fencing equipment brand to develop a foil handle that athletes can personalize for themselves. We were thrilled when we learned that James Davis, the youngest member of the British Olympic fencing team, was so happy with his personalized foil that he would be competing with it in the Olympics!

September 2012

A strong interest in Sugru has been building in Scandinavia. We agree to a partnership with some like-minded fixer entrepreneurs from Norway, Halvard, and Edvard, to promote and distribute Sugru in the Nordic region. They love Sugru and are passionate about the same stuff we are. It's fun already.

Late September 2012

The inaugural London Design Festival 'Design Entrepreneur' award goes to Jane! Woo hoo! After moving into the various worlds of science and business, it's awesome to be recognized for our creative vision and achievements by a jury composed of some of the most radical and famous designers in the world including Thomas Heatherwick and Ron Arad. I pick up the award at an exclusive ceremony in the Government building in Whitehall!

October 2012

Fix of the Month goes to an awesome teacher Matt and his class, who sent a camera up into space using a helium balloon. They use Sugru to waterproof their camera and secure it in place for its interstellar adventure. The photos are beautiful and remind us of a world of potential.

November 2012

Sugru has always been about so much more than itself. We felt strongly that we could help fuel a conversation about why a culture of fixing is important - so we made the Fixer's

Manifesto. It hit a nerve and was shared all around the internet. We printed lovely letterpress posters and made them available through the sugru.com shop.

January 2013

Sugru user Jamie, an expedition writer, and an all-around awesome person, sent us an email to tell us about his epic journey across Mongolia. He'd packed Sugru 'just in case' and found that it came in handy! Along the way, he patched up his boots, repaired a rafting paddle, and even fixed a favorite toy for a new friend.

March 2013

The dream from the start has been to be in everyone's kitchen drawer, as useful as duct tape and super glue. To get there, we need to get it into the big stores. We'd been trying for a while, and at last, we make a huge leap by launching in more than 300 B&Q stores across the UK and Ireland. Whoop!

We get excited and hire a donkey for our launch video. As we expand, the team keeps growing too. We welcome our latest recruit, Buddy. He's not very experienced, but he brings lots of energy and enthusiasm.

May 2013

I'd been getting a lot of invitations to share the story of Sugru at events and conferences. 99U at the Lincoln Centre in New York City was the biggest so far with 1,500 people, all tops of their fields in the creative industries. Other speakers included Joe Gebbia from Airbnb and Michael Wolff from Wolff Olins. I was so nervous that I did public speaking training for a few weeks beforehand. It paid off - for the first time, I enjoyed myself on stage. And when I finished my talk, the audience gave me the first standing ovation in the history of the conference. It was a moment I'll never forget.

With our expansion into retail getting off the ground in the UK, we set our sights on doing the same thing in the US, where half of our users had been since day one. We had another great year at the Bay Area Maker Faire, and the enthusiasm from our U.S. customers was infectious. Buoyed, we pushed on with plans to build out a small team in the U.S., as well as continuing to build the team in London.

August 2013

After 10 years together, James and I finally got married! If I hadn't met him back when I was a naive and excitable design student, Sugru would likely have been just another interesting student project that never made it beyond the college walls. With his support,

inspiration, and unique enthusiasm and vision, we have built Sugru into an awesome product and brand that people love. Now finally, he is my husband!

September 2013

While I was away, I'd had a nagging feeling something wasn't right back at work. And when I got back and met with the board, I was certain. Our costs and the team were growing too fast in relation to our sales and our management wasn't strong enough yet. Together with Roger and the board, we had to make some tough calls, and scale the team back by 30 percent. It was an incredibly stressful time for all the team, but we had to make sure we were building on strong foundations. Together, we needed to learn our lesson again. Start small and make it good.

October 2013

Roger co-founded the company with me back when I was just out of college 10 years back. We met for 20 minutes, clicked, and decided to start the business together. Ever since, he'd been the Executive Chairman, maintaining the vision through all those years while we worked in the lab. He'd helped build the team and raise the funding we needed, but now in this crisis was when Roger came into his own. James and I were tempted to scale back to e-commerce, without the costs that were needed to build our retail supply model. But it was Roger and the management team that kept the company on the right path. Focus on getting the business right for growth, keep going with the vision.

When I went to write the Community update that month, I found the stories they'd been sharing were more inspiring than ever. A surgeon in Haiti had used Sugru to patch up his mosquito net so he was sleeping better and doing better work. A group in Nairobi that invented the BRCK to bring internet connectivity to remote areas of Africa, told us they'd built the prototype with the help of Sugru. I felt a new connection with what Sugru could do.

November 2013

Despite all the tough work going on behind the scenes, Sugru was still growing and I'd been shortlisted for the prestigious EY Entrepreneur of the Year award in the Emerging category. We were getting stronger as a team, and this was something we could celebrate together.

December 2013

Sugru gets stocked in the Museum of Modern Art in New York City!

February 2014

We wanted to do something new and exciting for our users, and some of our favorite fixes involved pairing Sugru with magnets. We tested out lots of magnets and chose just the right ones to enable you to make pretty much anything magnetic. This was to be our first kit. We launched it on sugru.com and were overwhelmed with the response. We got pre-orders for 3,000 kits in the first week. People were excited. That's what it's all about!

April 2014

The awesome Science Gallery in Dublin asked me to help curate a show exploring failure. FAIL BETTER, named after Samuel Beckett's famous quote, asked 24 leaders in their fields to nominate inspiring stories of failure. Sir Ranulph Fiennes, Jocelyn Bell Burnell, Sonia o Sullivan, and Ken Robinson all contributed. Along with the original Beckett manuscripts, we made up a show that sparked lots of great conversations about the important role failure plays in creativity.

May 2014

By now people were mainly using Sugru for pragmatic fixes around the home -- fixing broken things that couldn't otherwise be fixed and solving everyday problems. These are our favorite uses for Sugru - because they're the most common and helpful to most people. But then, once in a while, an ingenious solution comes along that just puts a smile on your face. Sugru-er Andreas in Germany discovered that LEGO hands are the perfect size to hold phone charging cables! He mounted his LEGO on the side of his desk with Sugru, and hey presto - the most viral use of Sugru all year was born!

June 2014

The most common request from our customers had always been for longer shelf life. With a material like Sugru that transforms from one state to the next, just on exposure to the air, shelf-life is one of the most difficult things to achieve. When we started formulating Sugru, it was a miracle to get it to last 24 hours in the pack. With a lot of work when we launched Sugru lasted six months, then seven, then 10, and now after a huge amount of work by our tenacious R&D team, we were thrilled to bring it to 13 months in the pack. This was a huge milestone because it makes a big difference to lots of users and it opened up new distribution channels. High five!

July 2014

We set ourselves the challenge to make the most awesome water pistol ever with Sugru. The video we made about it got 1.6 million views in a week!

August 2014

Our expansion into retailers in the UK was going strong and we started expanding to stores in the US again. This time it was different, we had much more insight and experience now, and we were stronger as a team. Sugru-ers in the US were always asking to be able to buy Sugru in their local stores. Katie, our head of sales, and her team were happy to help!

October 2014

From an amazing shortlist, we won the London Living Wage Company of the Year award! As a company with ambitious business, including our factory, and one of the most important ways we can show appreciation is with the living wage. We were thrilled to accept our award from the Mayor of London Boris Johnson - and in return, we gave him a pack of Sugru!

November 2014

Sugru-ers love the color. For different reasons, some like to match colors and make their fixes blend in so they're almost invisible; others like their fixes to stand out, loud and proud. Either way, they all agreed on one thing, we should make Sugru in more colors. We expanded our range from five to 10, and people got excited!

The Fix of the Month came from Belinda. She wrote how her husband, who is blind, was not able to use the microwave when she was out at work. She thought about this, and how frustrating it was. Then she used her Sugru to solve the problem, by making the buttons tactile. Sugru-ers all have one thing in common - they are passionately independent, and they love to help others be more independent too.

December 2014

To help more people find Sugru in stores, and make it more distinctive and enjoyable, we re-designed our branding and packaging. Full colors on the foil packs help people know exactly what color is inside, the card wrapper gives more inspiration, and FIX THAT THING tells you exactly what Sugru is for. Our retailers and Sugru-ers both love it!

January 2015

We added almost 1,700 new stock locations in one go, as Sugru launches in Lowe's Home Improvement across the USA! We love to see our map filling up with these red pins.

April 2015

Our expansion into stores in the USA continues with Sugru launching in almost 2,000 Target stores across the country! This brings our total number from about 500 a year before to an amazing 5,000. In our mission to help people everywhere start fixing things again, this is a HUGE step - in both the UK and the U.S. now, a pack of Sugru is never far away!

For more information, please visit www.sugru.com

Terrafugia®... Driven to Fly™

By Team Terrafugia

Have you ever been stuck in traffic and thought why can't this car fly? -Robert Bear, InventionStories.com

While our ability to communicate and access information is increasing dramatically, personal transportation has not improved significantly in the past 50 years. If anything, travel today is more of a hassle. While the airlines have an impressive safety record, commercial air travel is far from convenient. Cars let you set your schedule, but they're slow and dangerous: the average commuter spends nearly five hours a week stuck in traffic, and globally, more than one million people die in car crashes each year.

We need the safety of commercial aviation, the convenience and flexibility of a car, and the freedom of the open sky. We need a new industry that makes personal aviation safer, as simple as driving your car, and convenient for everyone. We need a practical flying car. Terrafugia intends to lead the creation of a new flying car industry that will help humanity achieve this new dimension of personal freedom.

Terrafugia (ter-ra-FOO-gee-ah) intends to catalyze a revolution in personal mobility. Our vehicles bring a new level of safety, convenience, and freedom to personal transportation.

We have been dreaming about flying cars since the turn of the 20th century. The Transition® street-legal airplane is the first step on the road to the practical flying car. Terrafugia's vision for the future is the TF-X™: a bold concept intended to lead the creation of a new industry and bring personal aviation into the mainstream. We're starting with proven technology and our product roadmap is designed to make personal aviation progressively safer and more accessible to a broader segment of the population.

Terrafugia is derived from the Latin for "Escape the Earth". We're Driven to Fly. ™

Terrafugia was founded in 2006 to combine driving and flying in a new and practical way. Our founding team of award-winning MIT-trained aerospace engineers and MBAs are committed to making general aviation safer, more convenient, more fun, and more accessible.

We were one of three award winners in the MIT $100K Business Plan Competition in 2006. That summer, we launched the company publicly at EAA AirVenture in Oshkosh, WI where we met our first angel investors and received our first refundable deposits for the Transition®.

The Transition® is a two-place, fixed-wing street-legal aircraft that fits in a single car garage and is designed to be flown in and out of general aviation airports. It is designed to be easy and fun to fly and is extremely simple to convert between flying and driving modes.

Component and vehicle prototyping began in earnest in 2007. The Proof-of-Concept Transition® was successfully flown for the first time in March of 2009. Moving to our current 19,000-square-foot location in Woburn, MA in the fall of 2010, we accelerated prototyping and pre-production activities. In late 2011, the second-generation Transition® prototype entered its testing program. This second-generation prototype flew for the first time in March 2012 and conducted a live flying-driving demonstration for the first time that autumn.

Terrafugia made its debut outside of the aviation world at the New York International Auto Show in April 2012 for a crowd of more than a million attendees and continues to attend EAA AirVenture annually.

Terrafugia was also a subcontractor on a project funded by the Defense Advanced Research Projects Agency (DARPA) to do conceptual design and sub-scale system prototyping on the "Transformer X" program to develop a semi-autonomous dual-mode vehicle for the U.S. military from 2010 through mid-2012.

The Transition® is a Proof of Process for the vision for the future of personal transportation that we shared during the spring of 2013 by unveiling the TF-X™ concept. TF-X™ is a four-place vertical takeoff and landing (VTOL) hybrid electric vehicle that is designed to revolutionize personal travel as Terrafugia leads the creation of this new flying car industry.

By the spring of 2013, Terrafugia had grown from its initial founding team and three full-time employees in 2007 to more than 20 people on-site in Woburn, MA dedicated to the development, testing, certification, and production of the Transition® and realization of Terrafugia's vision. To learn more about joining Terrafugia in creating the future of personal transportation, explore our "Careers" and "Get Involved" sections, reserve a place in production for the Transition®, or visit our "Investor Relations" page.

Terrafugia's CEO/CTO and co-founder Carl Dietrich received his BS, MS, and Ph.D. from the Department of Aeronautics and Astronautics at the Massachusetts Institute of Technology (MIT) shortly after being selected as the 2006 winner of the prestigious Lemelson-MIT Student Prize for Innovation. Carl was additionally recognized by the Aero/Astro Department at MIT as one of 16 exceptional graduates under the age of 35. Carl has also received "40 Under 40" awards from the Boston Business Journal and Aviation Week & Space Technology magazine.

Carl has spoken internationally and is generally regarded as the leader of the emerging modern flying car industry. He has been a private pilot since the age of 17.

Carl shares his advice to those interested in inventing

The invention is about coming up with new solutions to problems that people have today. First, find a problem, then brainstorm creative ways of solving that problem. Pick the best solution you can, then invest the time needed to turn that idea into reality. That is the essence of making a useful invention.

But coming up with the solution to the problem is not enough. For the invention to matter, it needs to get to the people with the problem — this is the process of commercializing your invention. In my experience, it is often much harder for an inventor to commercialize an invention than it is to come up with the invention in the first place. But the second step is critical if you want your inventions to matter to other people.

It helps to find a fantastic team of people that recognize the value of your invention and are willing to help you commercialize it. If you want to be a real innovator, you think through the process of commercialization in detail before you invest the time in the invention itself — that keeps your focus on only the inventions that will matter to others.

For more information, please visit www.terrafugia.com

SnapIt Screw

By Nancy Tedeschi

The SnapIt Screw is a revolutionary way to repair your broken eyeglasses in 30 seconds

I invented SnapIt after my mother used a dangling earring to hold her broken glasses together. After creating eyeglass charms, I wanted to find an easier way to screw together eyeglasses so I reinvented the tiny screws that are so difficult to grasp. SnapIt's design uses a feeder tab that guides the screws in place with the use of clumsy fingers, snapping off once the repair is done.

When I was a child, I was the kid that everyone bullied. I had buck teeth and I was constantly called names like Bucky Beaver and Buck Teeth. Somewhere along the way, I detached from myself so I didn't have to feel the pain.

I barely graduated from high school when the counselors told my parents that I just was not a bright child. They gave me an IQ test and my score was 92. Seven years later, after graduating high school I applied to my local community college. They would not accept me unless I took some remedial courses. I took the classes and did very well then moved on to enroll in college. With my slow success in life, I began to develop self-confidence, and boy, did I soar!

I invented the SnapIt Screw (snapitscrew.com) and was able to bring my product from concept to the shelves of major retailers on my own. Only about one-half of one percent of inventors can say that they have done this. After college, I was given another IQ test and my score had risen to 146, which should tell you a lot about what confidence can do for you. I knew that I was not stupid and know that if I were not bullied throughout my life, that I would have not had the strength and determination to pull through. I believe that God puts us all in a place throughout our lives to use us in the best way he knows how.

I now understand why I went through what I did when I was younger and want to direct my efforts towards a greater cause, to put an end to bullying. While teaming up with Jaylen's Challenge, I have decided to give back and support this little boy who can be a voice for so many children. Jaylen has a message that has begun to spread and I want to donate a portion of net proceeds from my company to help Jaylen take this problem nationwide.

My company placed in the Top Three products for Walmart's Get on the Shelf contest in 2012. From April 11 to 24, consumers voted for the products that they would like to see on the shelves of Walmart. The grand prize was product placement in Walmart's all over.

While I understand the endless opportunities for my company if we were to win and get SnapIt Screw onto the shelves of every Walmart, I also see the endless amount of support that I could provide to different anti-bullying foundations, like Jaylen's Challenge, to help bring bullying to an end. With my support and the support from my company, I could help to fund some of Jaylen's dreams such as traveling to schools to speak about bullying and bringing an end to a problem that has been going on for far too long.

In life, you sometimes don't understand why you have to go through some of the hard times but I can honestly say that God had plans for me the day I was born. I would not trade my buck teeth for anything in the world and I hoped that with the same determination that I used to conquer my self-esteem, get my product on the shelves of major retailers that I can help eradicate the bullying that occurs every day in this country.

My Journey

I applied for a patent in August 2008. The examiner has made several mistakes which I was successful in getting overturned. It cost me an additional nine months in the system. I am receiving patents in foreign countries and struggled to navigate through the system in my own country.

I signed a license agreement with a big company to get my product on the market. Suffice it to say they did nothing for nine months at which time I canceled the agreement. I have been successful at putting the product on the shelves. Shame on me for not getting a more detailed agreement.

I paid a company that promised to help me get a company to back my product and make me lots of money. Of course, nothing ever transpired. I then paid another company $10,000 to bring it to the market and after four months, when nothing was done, I demanded my money back and moved on. Lucky for me, they gave it back to me.

Next, I negotiated a contract with an infomercial company that was supposed to be my "partner" and bring my product to the market. They were to come up with half the money and I would pay half the money, we would share in the profits. Again, after four months, nothing was done after giving them $7,500 upfront. Shame on me! They told me it would cost us $50,000; I would pay $25,000 and they would pay $25,000. After much research, I ended up producing and testing the infomercial myself for a total cost of about $12,000.

I am sure you are reading this and saying WOW how stupid can someone be? I would have to defend myself and say that I am a highly successful businesswoman. I have worked for myself for 25 years and I have a lot to show for it. I will say that the business I was in has nothing to do with being an inventor.

Trying to get a return call back from a buyer at a major department store is impossible. For every 100 calls, you make I might get one return call. My product works and makes fixing your eyeglass a cinch. Please watch my video at snapitscrew.com.

I tell people that I hate this screw and they laugh. It's not that I hate the screw because it does revolutionize the way we will fix our eyeglasses. But it is the process in which I hate. Through this process, I can say that I found my passion. I have given talks at the Manhattan Inventors Association, the Greater Wenatchee Area Technology Alliance Center. I have several upcoming speaking engagements at universities around the country.

My goal now is to help other inventors navigate their way through an impossible system. Quite frankly I don't care if I ever make any money doing it. I'm told that when you find your passion, it does not feel like work and that is how I feel.

Please help me get this story out to streamline this process which will help our economy recover and put people back to work.

For more information, please visit www.snapitscrew.com

Solve Life's Unexpected Marx

By Stephanie and Nancy Tomovska

Unmarx is the brainchild of sisters, Stephanie and Nancy Tomovska from Rochester Hills, Michigan

We invented our wardrobe must-have to help everyone look their best while helping wipe away cancer. After losing our mother to breast cancer, donating to this cause has been a personal mission of ours. We donate five percent of our annual proceeds to breast cancer organizations.

Unmarx, made in the USA, is a reusable cleaning pad with a chemical-free mesh that easily erases a variety of unexpected clothing marks from deodorant, lint, pet hair, makeup powders, baby, and body powders, dried food, dried dirt, dandruff, and more. Unmarx works without water and is small enough to take on the go. Not only is it functional but also available in a variety of fun colors.

The #1 question we always get asked is "How did you think of the idea for Unmarx?" The majority of ideas come from a problem. In everyday life, when there's a problem, we find a solution. Whether it is removing lint with tape or using a wet towel to remove deodorant marks. When we came across these everyday clothing mark problems, we thought there has to be a solution. After visiting many stores and searching the internet and not finding one, the idea came to us – we need to invent something!

Not knowing where to start when inventing a product or what the first steps are, we visited our local library and found an inventor's handbook to help map out our action plan. We formed our business entity, gathered and requested material samples, constructed a prototype, and found a local manufacturer. The library became our office and the librarians became our informal focus group.

But with every plan, there are always some obstacles. One of them we came across was sewing. Sewing is the glue to our product. Neither one of us knew how to sew so we bought our first sewing machine and tested our skills. A few broken needles later, we realized we needed to get some professional help to make our product look market-ready.

Another obstacle we encountered was getting people to believe we were a viable company and open for business. We overcame this by reaching out and introducing our product to media outlets (TV, print, radio, and blogs). By having the media cover our story, we gained the exposure and credibility that we needed to reach a mass audience and increase our sales.

We currently sell our product Unmarx in more than 80 Walgreens, Whole Foods Market, Ace Hardware, boutiques, yoga studios, and pet stores.

We are on a mission to Unmarx everything in the world. By popular demand, we will be expanding the Unmarx line to include your home and automobile.

For more information, please visit www.unmarx.com

Tired eyes can't see the Needle Eye? Get the Spiral Eye™

By Pam Turner

I remember laughing as my mom struggled to thread a needle

Glasses resting on her nose, she trimmed the end of the thread, sucked on it, failed to get it through the eye of the needle, and re-trimmed it. Sometimes she would curse, "Why can't someone invent a better needle? We've been to the moon, for goodness's sake."

Eventually, she would break down and ask one of us kids to thread it for her.

Then, just a few years ago, I realized it was me that couldn't get a limp piece of thread through a hole I couldn't see. And it wasn't so funny. My mom died in 1976, but I could hear her laughter as I struggled to get that needle threaded.

Surely someone had invented a better needle by now. So, I went shopping for one. I found an open eye needle called the calyx needle (it has an opening at the top.) It was easy to thread, but the thread came out every time I used it. I tossed the needle in the trash. No one was ever going to invent a better needle.

Forty years is long enough to wait for someone else to do something. I decided it was up to me. So, I did it. I did it for Mom. I did it for all the moms.

My mission: Change the world.

How can I think a needle is going to do that?

My little needle is going to be of no interest to a large majority of the world, but for those who need it, the Spiral Eye Needle is going to matter. A lot. Maybe it means a savings of a few seconds threading a needle to some people, but to others, it represents independence because they will be able to mend their clothes without help.

It means the Baby Boomer who can barely thread a needle herself won't have to pre-thread needles for her mother when she visits. It means the soldier that came back from Iraq with one less arm or only one eye will be able to sew on his button. Even blind people sew, and this needle makes it easier for them. It means the stroke victim can retain some dignity and a little more independence.

For crafters, the Spiral Eye Needle means they can spend more time enjoying the part of sewing they enjoy.

For anyone who has a snag in their shirt and can't get it back through the material, the

Spiral Eye Needle allows them to catch the stray thread and sew it back in effortlessly.

To those women in third world countries, without electricity or optical care insurance, whose hand needlework is under-appreciated by the world, it means their job will be just a little easier, just a little more efficient, and they will be able to do it a little longer, bringing in more money for their families, thus giving them a stronger sense of self-worth.

On a larger level, because I will only manufacture my product in the USA, it will mean people here will have jobs.

It means my customers will know the product they are buying isn't going to show up on the news as being tainted with lead or mercury. And, hopefully, it will encourage other startups to stay in America for their manufacturing needs.

If some child sees my needle and realizes simple little inventions are important as big, complicated ones, and that there is nothing that can't be done, I will have changed the future.

I'm an impatient person who got tired of the minor inconvenience of threading a needle. Putting an opening on the side seemed so obvious to me. Why hadn't it been done? My stubborn streak intensified every time I was told it couldn't be done.

When I went to the hardware store and discovered innovative tools and screws, I got just a little angrier, a little more determined. I'm not a metallurgist or an engineer. It took me years of frustrating conversations with the tool and die makers, and others in the metal manufacturing industry to learn the "why" it hadn't been done before.

Along the way, I learned some history too. Making sewing needles was an art lost to Americans in the colonial days because the only person who knew how to do it refused to share his knowledge. Today, needle making is a very protected process, done mostly in China and India, with some needles made in England and Germany. I have yet to find a company in America that manufactures hand-sewing needles.

When I came up with my idea of a side-threading needle, I quickly learned I needed a prototype so I started calling phone numbers of metal shops. All of them told me it "could not be done" or "people won't pay what it costs to make it." To which I would respond "Why not?" then "Can you recommend someone who might be able to help me?" The next call I made started with: "So-and-so suggested I call you." I used these exact words the first caller had defined as the obstacle in manufacturing.

After weeks of cold calling, I got Chuck on the phone, "Well, I suppose I could cut off the eye of a needle and cut it with an EDM." "Of course," he warned me, "it would cost a lot more than a regular needle." I had no idea what an EDM (electrical discharge machine) was but that was exactly how I made my prototype. And they worked! Not perfectly, but my concept was solid. Unfortunately, they could not manufacture.

Chuck referred me to Tom, a one-man prototype shop. Tom took me seriously, unlike most of the others. And he spent the time to help me others would not give. But in the end, he determined I would need to find a metallurgist. He had no one to recommend.

So, I called back those people I had talked with until I found one who knew a metallurgist. "Tell him you need 'precipitation hardening stainless steel.' It will make you sound like you need to be taken seriously." I had no idea what that was either.

The metallurgist did take me seriously. He met with me and looked at my drawings and my initial prototypes and came up with a metal that met my needs. He also was so excited about my concept he offered to help me get tooling done to make them. He was very experienced and had a vast knowledge of needle making. I believed him when he told me that he would have 30,000 needles made for me by Oct. 15, 2007. I gave him my life savings and quit my "real job" on Oct. 7, 2007.

I was so confident in this arrangement I had even managed to get a booth at the 2008 Minnesota State Fair. But, after November and December passed, it was obvious I had a big problem. I had a whole bunch of eight-foot lengths of precipitation hardening stainless steel and a handful of tooling parts of some kind, but not a single working needle.

I went back to Tom. After several failed attempts of trying to create a tool and process for manufacturing, we had to admit defeat. He could think of only one company that might be able to help me. So, the next day I sat in a conference room with the father and son who owned a high-precision manufacturing shop. I showed them what I had. Told them about the booth at the fair and that I estimated I needed 30,000 needles in time for that.

Can you make the eye? "Yes."

Can you have 30,000 made by State Fair in August? "Yes."

Okay, here was the big one. "I won't be able to pay you until we are up to production levels."

Dad looked at the son then the son looked at dad. I could feel the "No" in the air. But before they could respond, Mom stepped into the room and picked up my prototype, and said, "I need this." And the deal was done.

Of course, there was one small manufacturing problem. They couldn't make the point. Only the eye. And the point had to be made second because they couldn't put the eye in using their current equipment if the point was there.

No problem. I would simply grind the points after they put eyes into little pieces of the wire I had.

I thought there would be something like an old-fashioned pencil sharpener to put points into wire. There wasn't. I finally bought a small grinding wheel. The first time I used it, the needle flew out of my hand. That wasn't going to work. Back to the store to buy a slow wet grinding wheel.

This worked better but getting that rounded even tapered cone shape of a needle point was hard to do consistently. So, I bought a Dremel tool. With that little piece of wire inserted into the Dremel, my potential needle spun in the opposite direction of the slow wet grinder. Pressing the spinning wire in the Dremel against the stone wheel of the grinder produced a decent point. I ground points into needles for hours. For days. For weeks. A deep groove circled the stone from grinding so many needles.

The state fair was only a few months away and thankfully my handmade prototypes worked well enough. I sewed on a button and fixed a pair of jeans with it. I bought popsicle sticks and felt dots and would sell "Needles on a stick" at the fair. It worked! After the fair, I knew my needle could be made. And people would pay what it cost to make them. It wasn't a lot of profit, but the costs would go down with volume. I was sure of it. I had a working prototype out there. People had my website information. I had a manufacturer. I was a business.

In the beginning, I sold at sewing and craft shows and state fairs and expos. Direct consumer contact was invaluable in improving my needle. For example, the left-handed users had trouble with the prototype needle-catching material, but right-handed people did not. I am right-handed. All my testers were right-handed. If I hadn't had user input at the early stages I would have failed in the mass market.

At the Minnesota Inventor's Congress Invention and Ideas Show in Redwood Falls, I was among a room full of inventors. It was like I had spent my whole life an ugly duckling and suddenly found my flock. That was why I had never felt like I fit into the world. I am an inventor; I just didn't know it. In June 2008, I exhibited at the show. I knew I had a great product but had struggled so hard to get them made that I often questioned my sanity. Why did it seem so obvious to me, but not to others?

I earned a great deal of publicity through awards at inventor's events and hobby organizations. By networking with inventors and product development people I learned how to be in the right place at the right time. I managed to get on ABC Nightline and a Discovery Channel show called Pitchmen 2. I even got a worldwide exclusive licensing deal with As Seen on TV. Unfortunately, that prevented me from pursuing licensing with anyone else. Eventually, the As Seen on TV deal ended.

One day I found a knock-off of my needle being sold in a catalog. It was made in China, of course. When I bought them, I was not impressed. My patent allowed me to stop the sales of the knock-off. I then got an agent in China to purchase the knock-offs for me. I named them SENCH needles (Spiral Eye Needles China). They are profitable enough that I can wholesale and distribute them on a larger scale.

More information about the Spiral Eye™ Side Threading Needle at www.spiraleyeneedles.com

Budwrap - Wear Your Wires

By Mark Williams

The Budwrap is a silicone wristband that holds earphones

I'm just an average guy who was lucky enough to pursue my idea, starting in my kitchen with some oven-baked clay as a prototype. I hope you find some interest in my story and even some inspiration to follow your dream, whatever that may be.

I'm a graphic designer and digital media teacher in Texas. I've poured my blood, sweat, and tears into every step of the Budwrap product development. Boy, have I learned a lot! I hope that other inventors and entrepreneurs-at-heart will find inspiration in my humble beginnings on a limited budget. I believe that anyone can come up with a simple invention if they genuinely think outside of the box.

I guess you can say that I'm the stereotypical inventor who always tore that random gadget apart so I could figure out how the silly thing worked. I've always loved art, thinking creatively, and finding odd ways to make money. My mind is never satisfied with the idea that everything's already been thought of. There's always a new idea right around the corner just waiting to be discovered.

The idea of the Budwrap came after several weeks of realizing I needed to come up with something simple, but brilliant of course, to make money. In the past, I always had elaborate ideas for creating wealth but most of my thinking involved too much time, money, and risk to even think about taking the first steps. So, instead of buying a retail building and making it into a winter wonderland for Texans to enjoy (during the middle of summer), I needed to tone it down a bit. My thinking needed to be more realistic.

"Just a simple product, not too expensive to manufacture and easy to ship to someone's doorstep" were my thoughts. If only I could dedicate my mind to this concept and think about it hard enough, I could come up with an awesome idea! My mind was racing throughout the night and the next day just trying to think of something – anything – that could solve a common problem and make life a little bit easier.

Then one morning at the beginning of the school day (in my first year as a high school teacher), I walked from my car to the front of the school and saw many students wearing two popular things -- earbuds and silicone bracelets. Bingo! The idea hit me like a swift slap across the face as if the idea were staring me down the entire time. "I can re-invent the silicone bracelet to manage earbud cords!" And that very morning, the Budwrap was born!

Thousands of people claim to have the next million-dollar idea, right?

But most people don't act upon their "flash of genius" and just let the idea linger in their heads. Then you see one of those pitchmen on TV spouting everything off about YOUR idea. "But wait, there's more." I was bound and determined to never let this happen with the Budwrap, so I vowed to pursue this idea to the very end. And thankfully, that's exactly what I've been able to do.

From prototyping and design, talking with intellectual property lawyers, filing for patents and trademarks, dealing with manufacturers, and ramping up for production, to designing my own logo/packaging/website, it's been quite an unforgettable journey. And it's worth every minute of it! Even if I don't make a dime from my idea, it's still worth the education and satisfaction of knowing that I've followed my dream.

The Budwrap project was successful on Kickstarter.com so I went into the marketing and distribution phase of my little business.

Like most inventors, I didn't know where to get started so I made a few sketches, hoping to make sense of my jumbled thoughts. Then I made my prototype out of sculptor's clay and baked it in the oven to harden it. I've probably had at least 15 more prototypes since then. I used Google Sketchup, Adobe Illustrator, and Adobe Photoshop to create my first design renderings.

Then I found a reliable Solidworks designer on Craigslist to design my first 3D model of the Budwrap. It took hours and hours of trial and error and working with my Solidworks guy before I finally came up with something suitable for manufacturing. I thought, "Okay, the hard part is over and now I just need to get it manufactured." Hah!

There are hundreds of thousands of manufacturers for millions of different products and they are all manufactured differently. I knew my product needed to be injection molded, but I didn't know how to start or who to contact. After many, many quotes from manufacturers across the country and abroad, I finally settled on a plastics and rubber manufacturer that met the quality and standards that I needed.

Since I didn't know anything about the manufacturing process, I had to learn the lingo to communicate exactly what I needed. It's taken me more than three long years of design, redesign, two failed molds, and thousands of dollars to finally come up with a final design that works.

I have mass-produced more than 5,000 Budwraps. It's been a wonderful and challenging experience transforming the Budwrap– a simple idea in my head – into a tangible creation. But I'm still just another guy with an idea hoping to find success. I hope you can pursue your idea and find success too. Good luck!

TARPKLIP

By Lydia Woods

I'm the mother of three girls and grandmother of five in Fort Lauderdale Florida

I invented the TARPKLIP, a two-piece plastic clip for holding fabric without damaging it, allowing you to tie it down anywhere, making grommets obsolete.

The idea began as a "raft anchor." I needed something to hold an inflatable raft in the pool at the proper angle to the sun. When it came to the part to clamp on the raft, we couldn't find anything on the market. My determination led me to say, "I'll invent something."

We met a tool and die maker and worked together until we had a crude prototype.

It was during this process that we realized the clip had much more promise than a raft anchor. How big was the market? The fabric clip had such broad appeal for tents, boat covers, drop cloths, signs/banners, oh boy! Now we had to make an injection mold.

An acquaintance was a retired tool/die maker who still had a small shop. He fabricated a two-cavity mold for about $2,000. We brought it to a small injection mold shop and experimented with different plastic materials. We settled on a glass-filled polycarbonate, which is durable in both extreme cold and hot conditions and strong enough to offer a lifetime guarantee.

At the same time, we located a patent search individual who searched for a flat fee of

$200. A patent attorney wanted $3,000. The search showed no similar item so we decided to file a utility patent. We found an invention consultant, Pamela Riddle-Bird (author of Inventing for Idiots. She directed us to the patent searcher and a reasonable patent attorney. He was extremely helpful, agreeing to let us write the patent description and submit it on his letterhead. It came back, seeking clarification on a claim and professional drawings. The attorney took it from there and we had our U.S. patent granted in about seven months. To get foreign patents, we had to submit them within a year. We applied for Australia, New Zealand, Canada, Brazil, Europe, and Mexico at a cost of more than $20,000. We were successful in the first three, then gave up on the others. I have mixed feelings about foreign patents.

A friend of my daughters helped with a package design. We made some modifications and decided on a printed plastic bag, heat-sealed, that wouldn't take up much retail space. We did a limited production run and were ready to market the TARPKLIP, spelled like that to easily get a trademark. Another friend of our daughter's built the website. Also, we made an infomercial for about $2,000 and our New Zealand distributor made a great commercial. Both can be seen at www.tarpklip.com.

Shortly after the issuance of the patent, we got an invitation to attend INPEX in Pittsburgh. It's an international competition of 1,500 inventions. I entered three categories and won gold and bronze medals. I could have sold enough to pay for the trip, but we didn't have a state tax I.D.

Marketing is expensive, so I decided to try it myself. With a high school education and work experience of running a laundromat, I got off to a shaky start. Calling major retailers is tricky. I learned later that some of them found my enthusiasm to be "a breath of fresh air." I got an appointment with the buyer at Lowe's in North Carolina. They liked the product and were willing to try it in a limited number of stores. The problem was they required liability insurance for $5 million!! That's a high cost up front for limited exposure. In retrospect, I should have accepted but turned it down.

Free Advertising

My husband composed a press release and sent it to Popular Science and Popular Mechanics, Attn. New Products Editor. We had a post office box, which remained empty for quite a while. One day, a caller asked about the TARPKLIP. I asked where he saw it and he replied, Popular Science, in the new product section!! I went to the post office box and it was full!! Checks, cash, "send me some TARPKLIPS!!" The magazine doesn't inform you that it's accepted; they just print it. Sometimes, just your text and pictures, more often with their comments.

Our youngest daughter, away at college, continued sending press releases (use Bacon's directory to lookup industry publications with "New Products"). We eventually were put in dozens of magazines and that mailbox remained active. These magazines need products to fill their columns, so they give free advertising.

Our oldest daughter had a friend that sent out e-mails by the thousands all over the world. I had doubts but we got responses and orders from distributors in New Zealand and Japan. We saw the potential, so we had a 12-cavity mold made. Then we got lucky. A consumer saw it in one of the magazines and I suggested he bring it to a local store and I would pay him a finder's fee. He took it to Menard's Home Improvement Center. The manager loved it and referred it to his headquarters buyer. After much haggling, they placed an initial order of 27,000 packages worth more than $80,000!!! (They have more than 200 stores). I continued to ship a pallet of 2,000 packages every three or four months for almost five years.

We also had trial sales in several Walmarts. We tried QVC and Home Shopping Network, but they are looking for household items priced at five times the cost. I sold the TARPKLIP at the local boat and home shows with considerable success and consumer interest. Also, we met individuals that sold them to stores in Trinidad-Tobago and the U.K.

I still have some hardware and marine store customers, but the TARPKLIP has greater potential, especially the military. And it received Federal Emergency Management Agency approval. It performs better than anything on the shelves today. My limited efforts don't do it justice, so I'm willing to license it or sell it outright.

MADE IN THE U.S.A.

www.tarpklip.com

Appreciation

Thank you for reading Invention Stories...Tales from the Inventor. I hope you've enjoyed it.

If you are an inventor or have an idea for an invention, we salute you. One way to solve problems is to invent solutions.

If you've enjoyed this book, I'd like to ask you for a favor. Would you be kind enough to leave a review at inventionstories.com/book

I would greatly appreciate it.

Coming Soon...Women Inventors and the 7 Percent.

We invite you to visit our home page at InventionStories.com

Happy Inventing!

www.ingramcontent.com/pod-product-compliance
Lightning Source LLC
Chambersburg PA
CBHW060828220526
45466CB00003B/1016